21-Day

COUNTdOWN

to

Success

Take charge of your life in less than a month

By
Chris J. Witting, Jr.

CAREER PRESS
3 Tice Road, P.O. Box 687
Franklin Lakes, NJ 07417
1-800-CAREER-1
201-848-0310 (NJ and outside U.S.)
Fax: 201-848-1727

21-DAY COUNTDOWN TO SUCCESS
Cover design by Rossman Design
Printed in the U.S.A. by Book-mart Press

To order this title, please call toll-free 1-800-CAREER1 (NJ and Canada: 201-848-0310) to order using VISA or MasterCard, or for further information on books from Career Press.

Library of Congress Cataloging-in-Publication Data

Witting, Jr., Chris J.
    21-Day countdown to success : take charge of your
life in less than a month / by Chris J. Witting, Jr.
        p.   cm.
    Includes index.
    ISBN 1-56414-381-3 (pbk.)
    1. Success.   I. Title.
BJ1611.2.W55   1998
158.1--dc21   98-29119

To my parents, Grace and Chris Witting,
for showing me the path toward success.

Acknowledgments

Many people gave their valuable time and energy to the creation of this book. I owe a debt of gratitude to Brett Machtig, whose mentoring helped make this book a reality. Sincere thanks to my agent Jeff Herman, and my publisher, Ron Fry of Career Press, for their support. My editors, Nancy J. Witting, Audrey DeLaMartre, and Gloria Fuzia, performed superbly under deadline pressure.

Thanks to those whose ideas contributed to this book, including Susan Jeffers, Ph.D., Mark Victor Hansen, Lillian Vernon, Dr. Wayne W. Dyer, Bill Marriott, Herb Kelleher, Debbi Fields, Harvey Mackay, Bill Gates, Dave Liniger, Joe Tye, Victor Boc, Dr. Tony Alessandra, Wayne Allyn Root, Jose Silva, Greg Anderson, Nancy Rosanoff, Walter Anderson, Sonia Choquette, Tom Winniger, Elaine St. James, Ann Clurman, Terri Sjodin, Lama Surya Das, Nick Bunick, Dr. Robert Schuller, Dr. Norman Vincent Peale, Gerard Smith, David Maister, Faith Popcorn, Don Peppers, Dennis Wholey, Irwin Sternberg, Barbara Sher, and to the many other giants whose shoulders I stand upon, I am humbly grateful.

Many thanks to our radio listening audience. Without you, this book would not exist. My gratitude goes to the stations that air *Success Journal* and *Tracking Business Leaders*. Special thanks to Weezie Kramer, Julie Donohue, Amy Thompson, Lorna Gladstone, and Bob Dayton of WMAQ Chicago for their support from the start, along with Dan Mason of CBS. Thanks also to George Nicholaw and Bob Sims of KNX Los Angeles, Ritch Homberg and Ken Beck of WWJ Detroit,

Skip Essick and Stan Atkinson of WOOD Grand Rapids, Tim Farley of WRVA Richmond, Cliff Albert of KSDO/KOGO San Diego, Mark Larson of KPRZ San Diego, Duane Link of KEX Portland, Graham Satherlie of KRRF Denver, and all our fine affiliates from Alaska to the Virgin Islands.

To those who make our daily broadcasts possible, I salute you: Ken Williams, David Landau, and the team at Multiverse Networks, along with Roger Wolski at Radio Spirits. To the people who make my job easy, hearty thanks: Harry and Ann Remien, Jeff Barsch, Gary Dismukes, Dan Murphy, Jim Keller, Sandy Szafranski, Tim Smith, Geoff Rich, Steve Salutric, Richard Gayle, Josephine Vega-Adajar, and Mark Roth.

I'm grateful to the friends and family who inspired me along the way to complete this project: Gale, John, Karen, and Sandy Witting, for their support and understanding; Anne and Jim Kuhn, Lee Witting and Charlene Kent, Nancy and Charles Meyer, Chris (Sr.) and Marshia Witting, Carl Amari, Ron Rosenthal, personal coach Therese Kienast, Ardean Calloway, Steve Lessman, Kitty Weiner, Bill Latz, Susan Frank, Ellen Fader, Joyce O'Brien, Abby Polonsky, and Rick Starr. Last but not least, thanks to God for opening all the doors and to Guruji for his constant guidance.

Contents

Introduction

Not I, nor anyone else can travel that road
for you. You must travel it for yourself.

—Walt Whitman

21-Day Countdown to Success is unlike all other success books, because it does not pretend to offer you the magic formula for success. After years of doing interviews with and research on hundreds of successful people for my nationally syndicated radio program, *Success Journal*, I know there is no magic formula or single path to success that works for everyone. Actually, there are many different paths to success from which to choose, but only one that will work best for you. You could choose the same path as Debbi Fields, Bill Gates, or Lillian Vernon and yet never achieve their stunning levels of success. However, when you get on the path that's exactly right for you, you will see real results.

The many successful people you will read about in *Countdown to Success* were fortunate enough to discover their personal success path, and wise enough to stay on it until they arrived. If you have felt dissatisfied with your present course in life, perhaps you need to discover a better way. Most people spend their lives struggling along the same old road, wondering whether they will ever reach their dreams. The lucky ones discover there's a beautiful six-lane expressway just over the hill, created just for them. It's their personal path, ready and waiting to speed them to their dreams. This book was created to help you find *your* path. You will know when you find it, because your life will suddenly feel on course and your efforts will be fruitful.

Just as each of us has our own personal path, so do we each have our own definition of success. If you measure success in millions of dollars, you'll find one or more paths on these pages that will lead you to your goal. If a simple, fulfilling life—such as a life devoted to improving the planet and serving other people—is what you seek, that type of path is here to explore as well. Following the paths you will find here, you can discover success through career and business, through improved relationships, through mental focus, through spiritual growth and so on. Your role is to explore the paths, try them out, and choose as many as work for you.

Success isn't defined by the goal you seek, but by whether you reach it to your satisfaction. Which paths prove useful to you in reaching your definition of success will depend on your particular personality, what you need to overcome, and what you need to learn and understand. For example, do you need to stop beating up on yourself and learn to believe in your abilities? Do you need to overcome the habit of procrastination? Have you made your life so complex that you need to sort it out and simplify it to make it work? Is your self-doubt keeping your vision too limited? Is your dream big enough but do your financial habits keep you from pursuing it? Are you mired in the past? Whatever your problem, whatever your goal, you will find the tools to help you here.

Let me tell you how this process has worked for me. In the past my writing was limited. I never dreamed I could write a book. Nor did I believe I would ever have several nationally syndicated radio programs heard daily all across America. There are other goals I thought impossible that I have achieved recently, and many more that I am in the process of achieving. I was probably always capable of achieving these results, but I wasn't treading on *my* path in life, so everything was a struggle with little to show for the effort. Researching what worked for hundreds of successful people revealed several concepts that resonated powerfully within me. When I began to apply these concepts to my own life, wonderful things began to occur, seemingly by coincidence. Doors previously closed to me opened, and I achieved real results. I was amazed at how easily I moved ahead.

Other people you will read about on these pages used techniques completely different from mine and had similarly rewarding results. That's the point. In this book I offer you the means to sort through a variety of paths and to identify and begin to travel your unique path to success and satisfaction.

How to use this book

Today, as you begin reading *21-Day Countdown to Success*, your interest is high. You are eager to get rolling on your quest for success. But human behavior isn't constant. Most of us have "up" days and "down" days. Many who buy a self-help book in a moment of inspiration read a few chapters, then lose interest or get distracted. To help you stay motivated and get the full value from this book, I provide a 21-day countdown format. Why a countdown? Because what I call the Countdown Effect will power you forward day after day. Did you ever count down the minutes to midnight on New Year's Eve and feel the excitement growing? Did you ever stay glued to the television, watching the countdown to a rocket launch at Cape Canaveral? Or did you ever stay tuned to a radio station to hear the number one song in the countdown? Then you have experienced the Countdown Effect. It's real and it's powerful! And now you are going to use it to help you move through this program as you seek out your perfect path to success.

Should you miss a day or two along the way, just pick up where you left off and continue. Sample every path and explore every concept presented in the book. You will move ahead day by day, until

Day 1, when you achieve the peak of the program and you are ready to fly solo.

I have taken an outside-in approach, following the natural process of self-discovery: beginning with the exterior, worldly paths and moving to interior motivations and values. You may be surprised to discover which paths inspire and resonate for you. At the end of the Countdown there is a plan to help you select the paths you want to follow and additional resources to help you stay the course to success as you define it.

Do not rush through the program. Its effectiveness depends on your sampling each chapter fully, completing the written exercises and daily journal, and giving it a full day to resonate within you. If you feel compelled to read the entire book in one or two sittings, that's okay, but then take time to go back and follow the program from start to finish, one chapter a day. Ideally, you should do it at the same time each day. Allow time for the many different paths presented to work their magic on you.

Your daily journal

Your daily journal is an important part of the Countdown. It can take you as little as a few minutes a day, and it will truly help you identify your very best path to success as you move forward each day. Simply write—a few words or many, as you choose—something in each section of "Today's Journal" at the end of each chapter. Poor writing skills are no excuse!

Each day's journal contains the following four sections.

1. **What mattered to me today.** Note any part of that particular chapter that you found meaningful. Follow that with any meaningful or important things that happened during your day. If nothing seemed exceptionally meaningful, then think of the most significant moments and note those. Whatever you write may prove meaningful later when you view it in the context of the entire Countdown.

2. Coincidences, hunches, breakthroughs I experienced today. A coincidence is a sign that you're on the right path. Pay attention. Jose Silva, creator of the famous Silva Method of Mind Control, calls coincidences "divine intervention and guidance." So make note of any coincidences each day, large and small, so you can review them later. A *hunch* is your intuition. It is very personally yours and can be an indication that something in the day's path is valuable to you. If you have a strong hunch during the day, note it in your journal. A *breakthrough* is a sudden insight, a major problem solved, a new level of achievement—these will be important pieces of information when you evaluate the paths at the end of the Countdown.

3. New ideas I had today. Got a bright idea of any kind? Make a note of it here. New ideas can be further indicators that you have found value in this path to success, because they tend to happen when your thinking is at a high level. Also, it's good to capture your ideas in writing immediately, because they are easy to forget.

4. My thoughts, feelings, reflections on today. Make a note of your moods, your emotions, and your thoughts. It is also useful to include a word or two about relationships, career, and family in this section. Check your emotions. It's releasing to express them on paper, if only to clear your mind. If there is something you want to say to someone else but can't for some reason, write it in your journal. It's a healthy way to resolve matters.

There are specific benefits you will gain by tracking your thoughts, problems, and triumphs each day. Change is natural and constant. By capturing your changes day by day, you learn from them. Rereading today's thoughts a week, a month, or a year from now will reveal interesting things about yourself.

(If you prefer not to write in this book, you may order a separate 8½" x 11" *Countdown to Success Workbook and Journal* by calling 800-743-1988.)

How to enhance the effect

Here are a few tips to motivate you:

♦ First, notice the 21-day calendar on the next page. If you cross off the day on the calendar as you complete the day's chapter, it will accentuate your feeling of progress.

♦ Second, reward your progress with a small celebration as you complete each third of the countdown.

♦ Finally, plan a very special celebration for the end of the 21 days when you have completed the entire program. Write a brief description of your plans for this special celebration below the calendar to remind you of the fun ahead.

If you fully maintain your interest and involvement in the process for 21 days, you can discover your unique path to fulfillment and success as you define it. Make the commitment right now to support yourself and stay with the process. Take this challenge to reach for your dreams!

21-day calendar

			21		
		20	19		
18	17	16	15 One-third completed!	14	13
12	11	10	9	8 Two-thirds completed!	7
6	5	4	3	2	1 Final Day!

My celebration plans include: _____

_____

_____

_____

Think about it

*You plant a seed, water it, weed it...but you don't grow the seed.
All you can do is create the perfect conditions for the
universe to grow the seed for you.*

—Sonia Choquette

You must understand something as you begin this journey: No book will make you a success. In truth, no book, tape, or seminar on Earth can make you a success. The only way you can reach this seemingly elusive goal is by discovering and following your own personal and unique inner path. During my research and interviews with hundreds of successful people, many talked of having a hunch at a specific moment, or of being led in a certain direction, or of doing what came to them naturally. Some told about a burning desire to reach a goal, or a lucky break or a coincidental event that helped them succeed against the odds. After years of studying such people I've realized they were experiencing the outward signs of having found their unique, personal inner path, one that had previously been hidden from them. Once they got on their path, success came naturally and quickly for them.

Because you're reading this book, your inner path to success still may be hidden to you. Have no doubt, it is waiting to be discovered! All of us have within us a personal, inner path. This book does not offer the promise of a magic formula for success; rather, it provides a guidance system to your inner path that was previously invisible. Once you know what you are looking for, you will see it clearly. Once you recognize it, you will follow it as naturally as you breathe. As forks, turns, and obstacles appear on your inner path, guides and signposts will also appear, seemingly out of nowhere, to keep you moving in the right direction. The goals of success that were once out of reach will be accomplished in breathtakingly quick succession. Best of all, you will begin to feel fulfilled and complete on your journey toward success.

Promises, promises

At one time I believed, as perhaps you still do, that there exists a single, magical formula for success. Many of the books I read over the years implied it. When I was 14 I read a popular book that recommended a firm handshake, well-shined shoes, and a written set of goals as the golden keys to success. So I wrote out a list of goals, developed a crushing handshake, and had the shiniest shoes in town. Soon I realized it wasn't working! Another book recommended being ruthless and doing whatever it took to defeat the other guy. That didn't work either. Other success books have insisted that a positive attitude, a certain set of habits, mental programming, or other formulas would lead to success. Over the years I read dozens of success books. A few of them helped some, but none contained the magic formula to jump-start my career, bring me wealth, health, happiness, or peace of mind. It wasn't until years later, after I had the chance to study many hundreds of successful people, that I finally learned the truth.

There is no master key

Every year new experts claim to have found the ultimate success formula. Some of these ideas may help some people, but only if they are in harmony with the seeker's natural, inner path to success. Given that there are six billion unique people on our planet, there have got to be at least a few billion formulas for success. How could there be one single formula for success, when each of us has unique strengths, weaknesses, needs, and desires?

The real secret of success is realizing that the key to unlock your personal success is tucked inside you. All you need to do is learn how to recognize and use it.

Find your personal path

This book is actually a map, a treasure map, with all the information you need to find the ultimate prize of lifetime success. Like any map, it has many different paths going in different directions. While each path has helped someone, and might come close to helping you, your path may not be here. Also, like any good map, it points out some of the major obstacles you may encounter on your journey, and it will help you overcome or avoid them.

Read every chapter, do each exercise, and explore each new path in the pages ahead. Predictably, one path will resonate within you. Very possibly you will respond strongly to portions of several paths. While studying a particular chapter, you may have a sudden flash of insight. You may have a personal breakthrough. A certain idea may stick in your mind after you put the book down. You may abruptly recognize the obstacle that has been holding you back; you may feel guided in a certain direction. When any of these things occur, realize that you have discovered something important about yourself. You are getting close to finding your inner path. At that point, turn to the Resources section on page 247 to help you explore further, and then follow through. With determination and belief, you will soon be traveling along your personal inner path toward success.

Start the Countdown

There are two ways to present any kind of information: straight up, or with a twist. I've discovered my success by often doing things a little differently, and the growth of my *Success Journal* radio program is proof that my unique approach works. I don't just profile a successful person each day; I make it a mystery in which listeners have to figure out what person or well-known company I'm talking about, which is revealed in the last few words of the program.

When I was in school, the teachers who held my interest most used a unique approach, and that's what I chose to do here. Most self-improvement books are too predictable to be effective for most people. People buy them, begin to read, and then get bored. They put the book aside, maybe try again, but in the end, the book is never finished. I want to help you stay interested, so I turned the process upside down, beginning at what normally would be considered the end.

Therefore, we begin on Day 21. The Countdown Effect builds power until Day 1, when with a surge of power and a focused mind, you have lift off! You're on your own journey to the stars.

The first path

We begin by exploring a well-traveled path to success: using thoughts to change your life. Of course, everyone uses thoughts to make things happen, but these aren't everyday, casual thoughts. They are the deliberate and determined use of concentrated brain power to achieve something. Your focused thoughts will create your reality. A lot of successful people use this skill on a daily, hourly, and even minute-to-minute basis. By consciously focusing their belief in results, they soar over obstacles and arrive at their goals.

The very first path to success that I recognized was the use of thought to create reality. At that point, I had not yet heard of Sonia Choquette, author of *Your Heart's Desire* (Three Rivers Press, 1997), a book about creating the life you want. Choquette has conducted self-discovery training workshops for more than 15 years. A series of re-markable coincidences led me to interview her, and I was intrigued to learn that she makes the idea of using thought to create reality the first principle of her workshop. Recently, she told me how she first dis-covered this path.

When I was in high school, I was 5' 8". [Because of my height] no one would ask me out. It didn't bother me until it was the year of the prom and everybody in my class was going. I complained to my mother, saying it was her fault that I was so tall.

"You created that," she responded.

"I did not create the fact that I'm tall!"

"No, but you created that you're being left out. Why don't you create a prince, someone who will take you to the ball?" she said and walked away.

It occurred to me that she was right. Instead of finding a solution, I only dwelt on the problem. So, I decided I would create a prince. Every day I added another element to his ap-pearance. He would look like David Bowie, and have style and class. I did this every day for three weeks. Three days before the prom he hadn't appeared, even though I focused diligently. I was disgusted. I felt duped.

I decided to give myself a consolation prize and went to buy a new pair of shoes. There in the middle of the shoe store was a fantastic pair of white rhinestone platform shoes with silver shoelaces and six-inch acrylic blue soles. As I turned over the shoes to check the price, a voice said, "If you buy those shoes, I'll take you out!"

Stunned, I turned around to see a six-foot-three, skinny guy with long blond hair, about 19 years old. There was my prince! I bought the shoes, he took me out, and he actually ended up being my boyfriend all through the rest of high school!

What you think, you will experience, Choquette says. The power of the mind to create reality, to literally change the world, is astounding. Look around you. How many things do you see that didn't even exist until someone created them? Before those things were created, they were thoughts in someone's mind. A human mind, believing in and focused on an idea or purpose, can change the course of history. So the first path to success is consistently focusing your thoughts on what you desire.

Beginning now, observe all your thoughts.

♦ Be aware of your thinking patterns.

♦ Amid your constant churn of thoughts, how often do doubts appear?

♦ How often do you dwell on what you desire?

♦ Do you dismiss your dreams as out of reach?

♦ How often do strong, positive beliefs of your success enter your mind?

Doubtful, dismissive thoughts mean you are centering your focus on the problem and what's missing in your life. Instead, think of positive solutions and your ability to get results. Practice holding onto your positive thoughts. Keep them at the forefront of your thinking. When negative thoughts intrude, brush them aside gently. If you do that every time a negative thought happens, you'll slowly replace the negative habit with positive thoughts of how you'll succeed.

Achieving the American Dream

Recently a survey reported that fewer than one in five Americans say they've achieved the American dream. That's less than 20 percent of the population. Also, the survey said that most people don't even believe the American Dream is within their reach. They even identified the obstacles they believe keep them from success. Sadly, most people believe the American Dream is just a dream!

On the other hand, successful people who follow this path tend to believe that anyone can achieve the American Dream, in spite of the obstacles, because their thoughts create success. If you're willing to believe in the power of your own mind, anything becomes possible. Your thoughts become your reality. If you are convinced that there are too many obstacles in your path to success, sure enough, there will be too many obstacles, and you will create failure. But if you believe you can overcome any obstacles, then you will find a way to overcome them. You will discover ways to change negatives into positives, and you will achieve success.

Consider the survey just mentioned. If you believe that success isn't achievable, the survey will reinforce your thinking. It will confirm your belief that there's no point in trying, because there are all those obstacles to the American Dream. But if you believe absolutely that success isn't limited to a favored few, the survey will reveal an opportunity: If so many people believe that there's no chance of reaching the American Dream, then fewer people will be competing with you.

Believe, and you will find a way. In the last few years, 900,000 Americans became millionaires. Certainly, many of these people were believers in success. Try telling them now that the American dream can't be achieved!

A thinking machine

Your mind is an incredibly powerful computer, a thinking machine. Your thoughts are the blueprint for your success or failure. The beautiful thing about the human brain is that with knowledge and discipline, you can program it for success. Experts on the human brain used to believe that the brain was hard-wired and relatively un-changeable. But today neuroscientists know that it's possible for anyone to unlearn old behaviors and learn new behaviors and more powerful states of mind.

New learning causes a physical change in the brain. When stimulated by new information, the brain cells (neurons) actually grow branches (dendrites), leading to new connections. For example, this occurs when you start believing, really believing, in your ability to achieve success. As you focus on these thoughts, your brain starts to build a new network of connections, changing the physical linkages in your brain. The new wiring helps you make that powerful belief become reality. With continued belief, day after day, those connections become even stronger and success becomes more accessible.

Powerful connections

Researchers at the National Institutes of Health in Bethesda, Maryland, learned a few years ago how rapidly the human mind can build new connections and linkages. As part of an experiment, a group of adults was taught to play the piano. Researchers measured electrically the changes in the neural connections in the brains of those people. After just five days of piano practice, the researchers found that the people's brains had tripled the neural connections in the part of their brains used to learn piano. That's right, tripled in only five days.

What was even more amazing was that a separate group of adults was given just one piano lesson and then asked simply to think about themselves practicing. In other words, they were only to picture themselves practicing the piano. The researchers were astonished to find that during the same five days, those people also tripled the number of neural connections in the same part of their brains.

Believe and you'll achieve

By keeping your thoughts focused on success, by visualizing success and believing that you can succeed, your brain will start building new neural connections to help you achieve your goals. It's these powerful connections within your brain that will allow you to think in new ways and help make your dreams become reality.

Let's explore that process right now, with your first exercise. Write three compelling reasons why you believe you can be successful. For example:

- ♦ I believe I can be successful because I am smart!

- ♦ I believe I can be successful because in this country everyone has the chance to succeed.

- ♦ I believe I can be successful because I have guts and I am willing to take risks.

- ♦ I believe I can be successful because I am willing to work hard and stick with it.

- ♦ I believe I can be successful because I am willing to serve others to the best of my ability.

You get the idea. Thinking about and writing down your compelling beliefs about success activate the thought process I've been describing. These activities get your mind started building neural connections to help you make your dreams come true. That is a primary reason for the written exercises in this book. This is your first chance to take action and follow through. So grab that pen and do it! In the following space, write three reasons why you truly believe you can be successful.

3 compelling reasons why I can succeed

1. _____

2. _____

3. _____

Keep your mind focused on these compelling reasons for the next 24 hours, and see if this approach resonates within you. When a doubt or concern pops into your head, remember what you've written. Believe you can achieve your dreams!

One day at a time

The longest journey begins with just one step, according to an old proverb. You've already taken the first step toward success. Stay with it each day. Keep in mind that great achievements happen in a series of small steps. Just as Michelangelo painted the Sistine Chapel with many small brush strokes, and the massive Great Wall of China was built one rock at a time, so it will go with your success. Today you began, and for the next 20 days, your daily steps will lead you to discover your personal and unique inner path to success.

You may complete the daily journal now or later today, just before bedtime. Keep this chapter's ideas in your thoughts for the next 24 hours. Just before you fall asleep, review this path briefly, then sleep on it! While you sleep your subconscious will continue to work on it. Tomorrow you should have a good feel for how much of it resonated within you. Ask yourself tomorrow morning if you feel compelled to learn more about this particular pathway to success. If so, make a note to review this chapter at the end of the Countdown. But don't stop! Remember, every path in this program is worth exploring, so forge ahead tomorrow, Day 20, and believe in your future success!

Today's journal

What mattered to me today:

_____

_____

_____

_____

_____

Coincidences, hunches, breakthroughs I experienced today:

_____

_____

_____

_____

_____

New ideas I had today:

_____

_____

_____

_____

_____

My thoughts, feelings, reflections on today:

_____

_____

_____

_____

_____

Discover your destiny

Finding and filling your potential is the doorway
to your highest experience in life.

—Greg Anderson

Welcome back! Yesterday you began your journey of exploration by learning one of the most basic secrets of success. When you did Day 21's journaling exercise, you started putting that secret to work for you. If you skipped doing yesterday's exercise, go back and do it today! It's not too late, and each day's brief exercise is essential to your quest. Be good to yourself and make the most of your time investment by doing each day's exercise before moving ahead.

When you get actively involved in this process, you become a participant and absorb the maximum benefit from the Countdown. Results do not come to passive observers. To achieve success, you must not only use your mind but take action in the physical world as well. As the Zen proverb says, even the most enlightened must chop wood and carry water.

Get involved to get maximum value

Once I owned a home with a swimming pool. Pool owners tend to be very popular on hot summer days. When guests visited my pool, the kids jumped into the water right away and started splashing, playing, and having a great time. The adults cautiously checked the water temperature with a finger or toe, fretted about messing their hair, and checked the other adults so they wouldn't be first in the water. Then, if all conditions were met, maybe they'd go for a swim. But they never seemed to have the same kind of fun the kids did.

Successful people have learned that there's a direct association between *involvement* and *value*. Strong involvement in work, in family, in personal growth, or in any part of life is what brings the greatest rewards. Limited involvement in any area brings limited rewards. The bottom line is that if you want to seek your unique path to success, adopt the unrestrained attitude of a kid at the swimming pool. Immerse yourself in your quest and get involved. Develop enthusiasm for exploration and participation. That's the way to real fulfillment.

What you are meant to do

Today's success pathway is *doing what you are meant to do*. Many top achievers believe that their success came out of following their personal destiny and fulfilling their life mission. Some describe it more simply, saying that they played to their strength, or did what came naturally.

Greg Anderson is the author of six books and the founder of the American Wellness Project. In 1984, he was diagnosed with lung cancer that had metastasized through his lymph system. A surgeon told him he had just 30 days to live. Because medicine couldn't help him, Anderson decided to help himself. He researched those who had survived a medical death sentence like his and discovered in case after case that every survivor had a burning, driving, overwhelming reason to stay alive. Everyone he studied who had experienced a miracle cure was fully committed to a purpose. Each knew absolutely that he or she was on this Earth with a mission to accomplish, and wanted to complete it. Anderson's search revealed to him that his own mission was to inspire others to wellness.

Today Greg Anderson is happy and healthy. His recent book, *Living Life on Purpose* (HarperCollins, 1997), is an excellent guide to the life-changing process of finding your mission, your personal purpose for being alive.

Two things are worth mentioning here. First, you may not feel that you were born on purpose or that your life has any mission at all. If that's so, I recommend that you pretend that you have a purpose and a goal and that you'll find it. In other words, "Fake it until you make it." There's a 99 percent chance that you will become energized, you will become a believer, and you will find your mission. Believe me, it is there.

Second, you may wonder if it is possible to change your life's work at this point. Is it worth the effort without the threat of mortal illness? Is it wise to upset your routine when you have a family to support, a mortgage to pay, a busy schedule, and all sorts of commitments to honor? Greg Anderson told me recently that limiting thoughts like these are common. He says:

> *People tell me that there are three things that stand in the way of capturing their mission. One is time. They don't have the time; they have too many obligations and their work gets in the way. Another is money. They don't have the money; they just can't do it. The third is courage; although they know they should do something, they don't have the courage.*
>
> *Frankly, the one to focus on is the third: courage. There's always a way to find the time, and if the mission is right, the money will be there. The issue is to have the heart and the courage to move ahead, to have the courage to take one step forward and know that will open up doors to new levels of well-being.*

As Anderson suggests, suspend your self-limiting beliefs and give yourself the freedom to reach for greatness. Believe that you have a purpose. Everyone does. Surround yourself with people who share your convictions and limit your time with those who don't. Make your decision boldly. You will discover incredible new opportunities, and you will be delighted to find that the universe suddenly will start providing you with what you need to keep going.

Discovering your life's purpose begins by understanding where you fit into humanity. As a human, you are connected on many levels to everyone else on Earth. There are things about you that are unique, but you are more like others than you are different. You share the same biological structure, and you have the same basic emotions and needs as everyone else. Nonetheless, you are a unique individual. Understanding and developing your individual qualities can help you realize your destiny.

There's only one you

Genetically, you are unique. No one has ever had your exact genetic makeup. When your mom told you that you were special, she was right! Your DNA, the genetic blueprint in each of your cells, is as unique as your fingerprint. This genetic pattern developed through the combination of your parents' DNA and all of your countless ancestors. But your genetic uniqueness isn't the only way you are different from everyone else.

From your birth to today, you have been shaped and molded by countless random experiences. What you have learned, whom you have known, where you have lived, and what you have done have all contributed to your uniqueness. Every person in history has been a one-of-a-kind like you, with his or her own God-given unique combination of strengths and qualities.

Once you realize this, it is easy to see that there's a single best path that you alone can follow to achieve your greatest success. There is a purpose for you! It's there and it exists; all you need to do is discover it. In other words, *there's something that you can do that will take maximum advantage of your unique skills, talents, and abilities to provide the greatest service to others.* Serving others is a vital part of realizing your purpose in life and it is a major path to success. We will explore this path in detail later in the Countdown.

The eagle soars because it was born to fly, but no matter how hard you flap your arms, you won't fly. However, you can soar and achieve your ultimate goals if you do what you were born to do in life. Never have I heard this concept expressed as well as the way Walter Anderson, editor-in-chief of *Parade* magazine, stated it to me recently:

> *Destiny is not something we wait for. Destiny is not something that happens to us. Destiny is a choice, and we can choose to be the people we want to be.*

Open your mind

What were you born to do? As you try to find your way, you ask others for help and accept their advice because you don't know what else to do. Your parents, friends, mentors, and teachers try to help. You read and hear messages from various media. Maybe your choices are limited by economic or personal reasons, so you do the best you can. As a result, you may not be taking advantage of your intrinsic talents, and you may fail to achieve your greatest potential. At this point you may have other considerations, like a 20-year track record in a career, a mortgaged home, or a child depending on you.

Without a doubt, you have responsibilities, and that will always be the case. Nonetheless, no matter where you are now, you can discover ways to apply your natural talents and abilities more powerfully and achieve greater success. Don't just assume your life must remain as it is. Break free of limited thinking and focus on the infinite possibilities of the future. Remember, each day is a new beginning.

Unlock your potential

It is possible for you to achieve a measure of success without doing what fits your unique skills, of course. Right now you may be using some of your natural abilities. But you will achieve the greatest satisfaction, you will get the most out of your lifetime, and you will be most likely to realize your personal destiny if you do what you do best. One way to know if you're on the right track is to ask yourself if your occupation excites, fulfills, and satisfies you. If not, then it's time to find out what you could be doing to fit who you are. When you do that, you will unlock your highest potential.

"Don't die with the music still inside you," someone once said. When you sing your inner music born from your particular combination of abilities, you share with the world your sweetest song about the best of yourself.

Talk to yourself

One way to uncover your personal destiny is to ask yourself the following questions:

♦ What do I do best? What are my natural skills and abilities?

♦ How can I take the best advantage of this unique combination of strengths to earn the greatest rewards?

♦ Where and when do I begin?

Let's begin the process now. To begin identifying what you are meant to do and what you were born to do, name some things you do as easily as breathing. What skills, abilities, and talents do you use without thinking, because you enjoy using them? What do you love to do? For example, if you had a week all to yourself with no commitments and no plans, what would you enjoy doing most? Don't think only of work. Think of what you enjoy.

Another way to think about this is to consider the ways people compliment you. For example, maybe you have done a great job of decorating your home, and you receive many nice comments about it. Maybe you are a wonderful cook. Maybe you have a good memory for batting averages and sports facts. For example, Mike North had a hot dog restaurant in Chicago. His red hots were delicious and the place was successful, but what he really loved to do was talk sports. A few years ago he discovered his true calling, and today he co-hosts a popular radio sports talk show that entertains and informs thousands of listeners each day. Is there a hobby or pastime that you really enjoy? Is there something that you truly feel passionate about doing? Passionate is a good way to describe the feeling you will have about whatever it is you do best.

The daydreamer

A book written by Dale Pollock called *Skywalking* (Harmony Books, 1983) tells the story of a young boy's passion for reading comic books, watching TV, and going to the Saturday matinee. His favorite activity was daydreaming about fantasy worlds. It seemed like a foolish waste of time to others, but that boy grew up to achieve incredible success by pursuing his passion. Of course, I'm talking about George Lucas, producer of some of the most successful motion pictures of all time, including the *Star Wars* and the *Indiana Jones* trilogies.

Do what you love

Think of the people who are really successful at what they do, who have set the standards of excellence in their fields. Michael Jordan, basketball superstar of the Chicago Bulls, is clearly someone who succeeded by doing what comes naturally. Bill Gates, founder of Microsoft, became the youngest billionaire in America the same way. In an exclusive 1996 interview, Gates told me the simple reason for his success:

> *Certainly for me, I did what I enjoy doing. Because I loved it, I worked hard and got into a lot of depth, and got a lot of friends who felt the same way. So picking something that you really like, at any level of success, is the best choice.*

A common path shared by many top achievers is their use of their natural abilities, doing what they love to do. Marsha Sinetar expresses the concept so well in the title of her book, *Do What You Love, the Money Will Follow* (DTP, 1989).

Five natural abilities

As I write these words in my 30th-floor office, a tiny spider outside my window is spinning a small, perfect web with incredible efficiency. Random gusts of wind don't hinder the insect's progress because it is doing what comes naturally, what it was born to do. Like the spider, you have talents and abilities that you use without thinking. Take a few minutes now to list five of your natural abilities and aptitudes. Do not think about it too much or overanalyze. Do not worry about what it is leading to right now. Just jot down five things you enjoy doing most.

5 of my natural abilities

1. _____

2. _____

3. _____

4. _____

5. _____

How can you use your abilities?

Next, ask yourself, How can I use my unique skills to get maximum results? For example:

♦ If you love to write and you love to make people laugh, maybe you could write comedy for television, pen a hilarious novel, or even create a Broadway smash.

♦ If you love being outdoors and enjoy working with your hands, you could become a landscaping artist to put beauty into the lives of others. You could delve into herbal medicine, or become a farmer and feed the hungry.

There are literally thousands of choices in every general field, but only one that's best for you. It's important, however, not to hone the point too fine as you begin your search. Begin in general and work to specifics. As you sort through the many possibilities, remember the words of St. Francis: "Have patience with all things, but first of all with yourself."

What is your mission?

As you consider your unique combination of natural talents, consider also what major accomplishments would give you the greatest fulfillment while serving humanity. This involves the creation of a set of lifetime goals, what some call a "life mission." Your mission statement flows from your natural abilities and clarifies how you will serve others through the outward expression of your uniqueness. Your mission statement describes a broad vision of what you believe you are destined to accomplish in this lifetime. For many, such a statement reflects a spiritual point of view stating the role they believe God has given them to fulfill on Earth.

During my radio interview with Greg Anderson, he challenged listeners by saying:

> *Only about 11 percent of people who call themselves seekers have a personal, written mission statement. Now, if you're among that 11 percent, bravo! Congratulate yourself, you're on the road. But if you're among the 89 percent who don't [have one], I put a challenge to you today. Carve out an hour of quality time. Get out a piece of paper and start to draft a personal mission statement. Give it your best thought.... I can personally testify that there are tens of thousands of others whose lives have dramatically changed as a result of getting clarity on that mission and writing it down.*

In creating your mission statement or statement of purpose, look at the big picture. Have the end result in mind. What accomplishments would fill you with the most satisfaction when you look back someday? Don't let this process intimidate you. Your statement may end up as basic as:

> *My mission in life is to use my special talents as a parent and teacher to raise my children to be happy, healthy, peaceful souls who will help make the world a better place for everyone.*

or

> *My mission in life is to use my skills as a composer and guitar player to create music, providing peace and harmony that uplifts and enriches the lives of others.*

Remember, you're not carving this in stone. You can change your mission statement anytime and as often as you want as your life changes. However, having a written statement will provide clarity for you and will help sustain you when life gets confusing. Having a clear understanding of your natural abilities, and creating a life-mission statement for yourself may well be your personal pathway to success.

Think in unlimited ways

Though your mission statement may be uncomplicated, don't be afraid to reach higher than you have in the past. Here's the reality of what I have witnessed time and again in my personal and professional experience: Usually people create a lifetime mission that *does not do justice* to their capability and potential. Rarely do people give themselves a challenge that is too big or too ambitious. So, do not aim too low; do not underestimate your own God-given ability to achieve great things.

Make no little plans

Daniel H. Burnham, the legendary Chicago architect and city planner once wrote, "Make no little plans; they have no magic to stir men's blood.... Make big plans, aim high in hope and work." The size of Burnham's thinking has lasted more than 100 years, and will probably last hundreds more. What makes people successful, and what leads us to remember certain people as great achievers and contributors long after they're gone, is usually the magnitude of their thinking. Any goal that is within reach of another human being is also within your reach!

The irony is that most people find the big accomplishments of others perfectly reasonable. A movie actor or rock 'n' roll singer earns millions of dollars, and people don't give it a second thought; a small business launched in a garage grows into an empire, and people accept and applaud it; an athlete becomes a world champion and a role model to kids everywhere, and people cheer him; but when it comes to their own lives, their thinking suddenly becomes limited—they think small.

The wonderful thing about a challenging life mission is that it has the power to energize, motivate, and excite us, to help us accomplish more than we imagined possible. Small quests don't stoke the fire within us. Big thinking helps us envision a big mission, which in turn creates massive amounts of enthusiasm and inspiration to make it happen.

If you truly want success, if you honestly want much more out of life than you've had in the past, then you must have the courage to stretch your mind to its very limits. If your dream takes you to point A, stretch beyond that point to A plus B. In other words, make your belief in yourself bigger than it has been in the past. As you read, your thoughts and ideas are starting to expand. For the following exercise, keep your thinking wide and unlimited, and your mind open to new horizons.

Now, begin!

Imagine that your life has no limits. Let your mind go free right now. I want you to imagine, with no limitations whatsoever, achieving the goals that until now you have only dreamed of achieving. This is not the time to think small. Idealize your perfect future. Do not assume anything in your life has to be the way it is right now if you don't want it to be that way.

Your assignment is to follow through today and create a mission statement, using the list of natural talents and abilities you've already written down. Discover your personal destiny, as you explore this path toward success. It may well prove to be the most valuable investment of time you will make in your life.

My mission statement

_____

_____

_____

_____

_____

Today's journal

What mattered to me today:

_____

_____

_____

_____

_____

Coincidences, hunches, breakthroughs I experienced today:

_____

_____

_____

_____

_____

New ideas I had today:

_____

_____

_____

_____

_____

My thoughts, feelings, reflections on today:

_____

_____

_____

_____

_____

See your success

Visualizing is realizing—what you see is what you get.

—Mark Victor Hansen

You are moving forward, exploring new pathways to success and the effort you are making each day is a direct investment in your future. Reaching Day 19 of the Countdown shows your commitment to your personal growth. You are well on your way to finding your best path. If you're like most people, by now you have a sense of involvement and accomplishment. Stay with it. Discovering the pathway that works best for you will absolutely change your life for the better.

The power of visualization

The path to success we will explore today is visualization, a highly effective tool. Visualization is what we do when we daydream. Those who use visualization purposefully to get results create a picture of their goal in their mind and keep that image fixed on the mental screen using various methods. Thus, with their goal always in sight, they can turn the image into reality. This chapter explores the process of focused, intense, and deliberate mental picturing, which is far stronger than ordinary daydreaming.

A few years ago, Mark Victor Hansen and Jack Canfield co-wrote the book *Chicken Soup for the Soul* (Health Communications, 1993). It's filled with true stories of ordinary people doing extraordinary things, and the tales are uplifting and inspiring. Hansen and Canfield used visualization (plus another path we will explore tomorrow) to make their new book a success. They decided to visualize their book reaching the number-one spot on *The New York Times* best-seller list, certainly a true measure of publishing achievement. To help them picture it clearly, they clipped out a best-seller list from the paper, removed the title in the number one spot and pasted their book's title into that position. Both men put copies of that altered best-seller list on their office walls so they would see it every day. In addition, they pasted the words *"New York Times* bestseller" on the cover of a few copies of their book, which they kept in plain view.

Visualization, assisted by these props, was effective for them. Recently Hansen told me that their book, which was originally rejected by dozens of publishers, had been on *The New York Times* best-seller list for 129 weeks. *Chicken Soup for the Soul* and its sequels have sold more than 60 million copies. Though Hansen and Canfield helped their visualization along by creating a fake best-seller list and a doctored book cover, it is not necessary to create such physical objects. Most people who use visualization successfully simply picture in their minds what they want to achieve, and use that mental image to coax their desire into reality. The use of props is just icing on the cake, albeit very tasty icing that might help keep spirits high.

What's behind visualization?

How can something as simple as visualization be so effective for some people? No one knows for certain, but scientists offer a probable explanation of what happens in the mind during visualization.

Consider that when you look at a physical object, such as a chair, your eyes focus an image of that chair onto your *retinas*, which act like miniature television cameras. Your retinas transmit electrical impulses of the image of the chair to the part of your brain called the *visual cortex*. In this extremely complex area, containing billions of neurons, the data is processed and you recognize the object to be a chair. Finally, this information goes to the complex upper portions of the brain, where the mind analyzes the data so the body can respond with the appropriate action, which is to sit on the chair, walk around it, move it, etc. This amazing process of recognition, thought, decision, and response takes only a fraction of a second and is one we use continuously and take for granted.

Some brain researchers believe that when you visualize a goal or plan, you use the same process as I've described above, *only in reverse*. Consider, for example, that your goal is to build a new home in the mountains and you have decided to visualize that goal. This time the process *begins* in the upper part of your brain. Your complex, upper brain sends descriptive information about your goal downward to the visual cortex, where it is processed. The visual cortex is where you visualize your house.

Once this recognition and visualization process happens, the image of that goal on your mental screen begins to link new thoughts and ideas in your brain, all related to that single goal. You may develop what's commonly referred to as a "one-track mind," so that everything you do and say relates to your ultimate goal. Because so many of your thoughts and actions now revolve around that goal, it's logical to assume this intense focus will help you make it reality. Visualization has proved to be an effective path for seeking success, especially for those who might lose focus or get sidetracked without a visual image to guide them.

Results from visualization

There are many examples of people who have used visualization to achieve results. In one famous experiment, Russian athletes discovered that they attained their best performance when they spent three-fourths of their time visualizing desired results, and just one-fourth actually practicing!

Physicist and genius Albert Einstein said he would have been unable to achieve his breakthroughs without "mental pictures." He said that he created his theory of relativity only after visualizing himself running after and catching a speeding beam of light. He kept that startling image focused in his mind and eventually attained one of the greatest milestones in theoretical physics.

You don't have to be a genius like Einstein to use visualization. For obvious reasons, most people find it easier and more effective to apply visualization to a goal that's easily pictured. As Einstein commented, "Imagination is more important than knowledge." Being able to imagine your desire clearly can do much to make it happen. Examples of easily visualized goals include tangible objects such as a certain new car or home you wish to own, or seeing yourself achieve victory in sports or in business. On the other hand, if your goal is to earn a billion dollars, you may need, like Einstein, to create your own meaningful picture. Chicago Bulls superstar Michael Jordan is reported to have used visualization to manifest his record-breaking levels of performance on the basketball court.

You are what you think

Two days ago, you explored the fundamental concept that your thoughts can change your life. Inevitably, the first steps to success involve *applying the power of thought.* Just as nutritionists say "You are what you eat," in terms of success, "You are what you think." Your thoughts today create your tomorrow.

Visualization is an extension of the power of thought. Putting pictures on your mental screen and then concentrating on them takes the natural thought process one step further. Most people are visually oriented and can absorb and retain visual information more readily than spoken or written information. This is logical, given the large portion of our brain that's devoted to processing visual information.

Coincidence or visualization?

Dr. Wayne W. Dyer, noted author and lecturer, shares a personal story about the power of visualization in his book, *You'll See It When You Believe It* (HarperCollins, 1990). As a boy living in a modest East Detroit home, one of Dyer's favorite television shows was *The Tonight Show,* which at the time was hosted by Steve Allen. Dyer began visualizing himself appearing as a guest on the show. He told friends and family what he was going to say when he was interviewed. Although they laughed at him, the vision stayed in his mind. Years later he quit his college teaching job to pursue a full-time career as an author.

By the late 1970s, Dyer was on the road promoting his first book, *Your Erroneous Zones* (HarperCollins, 1976, revised 1991). After many months and hundreds of interviews all over America, his book hit *The New York Times* best-seller list. As you've probably already guessed, a producer from *The Tonight Show* called, asking if he'd come on the show to be interviewed by host Johnny Carson. Here's the amazing kicker: The night of his appearance, Dyer was waiting nervously backstage and decided to call his wife. He went to a bank of pay phones to dial, and who should be using the phone next to him but one of the other guests on that night's show, Steve Allen! Incredible coincidences, or the results of visualization?

Success or failure

Achievers who visualize are convinced that visualization is one of the most powerful paths to success—or failure! Yes, it can be a path to failure. Visualizing failure can lead you to fail just as surely as seeing images of success can help you win. It can make good things or bad things happen for you; it just depends on what picture you decide to hold in your mind.

If I tell you not to visualize a pink elephant, you will no doubt get a visual image of a pink elephant in your mind. In the same way, telling yourself not to visualize failure doesn't work very well either. Your mind, adept at creating pictures, will invoke a vision of failure faster than you can blink. What can you do? *Think success, always.* Keep a scene of success in mind for your brain to focus on. Should images of failure slip onto your mental screen, gently push them away and return to the image of your success goal. As Mark Victor Hansen told me:

> *You've got to hold on to that vision, because what the Universe does is test you, and it says, "No, that can't happen. Who are you, Mark Victor Hansen? You don't know anyone or anything. Get outta here!" You've got to see it inside, trust in it, have faith in it. You've got to see it before it can possibly happen. What you in-picture you out-picture. If you really picture the good you desire, whether it's a good family life, your business, a good relationship, visualization can make it happen. It's the inner work that causes the outer realization.*

Much of the effectiveness of visualization comes from creating an intense success image that burns into your brain. A casual visualization is like a fuzzy television picture. You need to focus the image, turn up the color and contrast and brightness, and make the picture so vibrant that it comes alive in your mind. This is the only way to discover whether or not visualization is truly your best path to success.

Visualize your future clearly

The more clearly focused and sharply defined your thoughts of success, the more effectively they can bring you to your goals. Crystallized, focused, almost palpable thoughts are the easiest to visualize, and therefore the easiest to bring into reality. The exercise on the following page will help you get your thoughts of success into sharp, clear focus. You will take a few minutes to write out a vivid description of how you might visualize your success. Remember, this is not a list of goals. Goal-setting is an important and exciting path we will explore later. Today, you are thinking about an image of your success.

First, how do you define your success? Achieving which of these desires would make you feel like you had become a success, financial abundance, a great relationship, a wonderful new job, perfect health, or total peace of mind? Imagine that you are watching a movie featuring you living a life of total success. Stop the movie and freeze-frame on the one image that best illustrates you enjoying ultimate success. Is it an image of you standing in front of your beautiful new home? Or you standing with your arms wrapped around a perfect someone? Or you sitting in your new Mercedes? Or maybe you sitting in your Mercedes, with your arms around a perfect someone, parked in front of your new home? Perhaps it's a far less material scene, an image of you experiencing complete peace of mind, simply enjoying life while surrounded by close friends and loved ones.

If you're having trouble picturing a scene of your perfect success, don't get hung up. For this exercise just choose a mental image that comes as close as possible to your definition of success. The goal is to test the effectiveness of visualization for you.

Okay, got that scene of success in mind? With that freeze-frame picture of success in your head, write a detailed, written description of that scene by imagining that it exists right now. In your mind, zoom in to see all the details. If the picture is fuzzy, just use your imagination to fill in the details.

The more visual your description, the better. Write down the exact color, texture, shape, and size of everything in your scene of success. Again, if you're not sure of certain details, make them up! Let go and explore this path of visualization. Describe your ideal picture of success vividly, allowing your mind to crystallize the image and to visualize all the details. For example, let's say that in your picture of success you live in a perfect home. Describe it. What is the style (contemporary, Tudor, etc.)? Write down its color, location (street, neighborhood, city, state), construction material (brick, fieldstone, etc.), its interior furnishings (oriental rugs over oak floors, abstract paintings on the walls, etc.), the number and type of rooms, the landscaping around the house (lawns with stately oak trees, etc.), and so on.

Let's say your perfect scene of success has you with the perfect someone. Describe his or her values, beliefs, appearance, and so on. Include any details that are important to you.

If your ideal picture of success has you in a new career, write in sentences a vivid description of your position, your title, your workplace, your salary, your benefits—even the values and philosophy of your new company, if you wish. If your goal is to own your own business, describe it in as much detail as you can.

Those are just some examples to consider. Use your imagination and picture vividly the perfect scene of your success and get it down in writing. Let your imagination go, because no one will read this but you.

My perfect image of success

_____

_____

_____

_____

_____

_____

_____

_____

_____

_____

When you've completed this highly descriptive paragraph that illustrates your success in one vibrant image, read it over slowly and visualize the complete picture you've created. Concentrate on the image of your perfect success, and see each detail in your mind's eye. Focus on every aspect of your scene. Dwell on this visualization and savor it for a few minutes, letting it imprint on your mental screen.

Visualize daily

To test the power of visualization, at least *once every day*, spend a few minutes reading this wonderful description you have just written of your ideal image of success. As you read it, concentrate. Visualize and dwell on the image, letting it linger in your mind. After a few days, decide if the image has become motivating. Notice if the scene pops into your mind during the day or appears in your dreams at night. You may find yourself being drawn toward people or activities that can lead you to this goal. You might start to notice unusual events or coincidences that open doors for you. Give visualization a chance to work and you may be surprised at how effective it is for you.

Avoid letting anyone else blur your perfect image of success by keeping it to yourself. Sharing your mental picture with others will invite their judgment and opinions, weakening the clarity and focus of your visualization. Give this tiny sprout a chance to grow in your mind without the intrusive thoughts of others. Your ideal picture of success is for you and you alone to enjoy each day, in the privacy of your own thoughts.

Art of mental pictures

Visualization may be what helps you achieve success. If it's right for you, you will find that its power to create reality is as unlimited as your mind's ability to imagine new goals.

That's it for Day 19 of the *Countdown to Success*. Tomorrow you'll explore a system for programming yourself for success. For now, if you haven't completed that written description of your ideal life, do it now and see how the power of visualization can work for you.

Today's journal

What mattered to me today:

_____

_____

_____

_____

_____

Coincidences, hunches, breakthroughs I experienced today:

_____

_____

_____

_____

New ideas I had today:

_____

_____

_____

_____

My thoughts, feelings, reflections on today:

_____

_____

_____

_____

Tell yourself to win

The most important words we'll ever utter are those words we say to ourselves, about ourselves, when we're by ourselves.

—Al Walker

Today, you'll explore the technique of positive affirmation, self-coaching, or what I call "Telling Yourself to Win." Is positive self-talk important? Yes. Does self-affirmation make a difference? Absolutely. Successful people give themselves daily positive feedback on their performance. Starting today, do it for yourself and discover how effective it is.

Drawing strength from affirmations

Scott dreamed of a different, more rewarding life, but he was stuck in a corporate job—until he found his pathway out. I've interviewed him twice, once by telephone and once in person, and asked him to tell me exactly how he reached his goals. Scott credits his success to his use of positive affirmations. Here's how he did it: Twenty times each day, he repeated a powerful, positive statement describing what he wanted to have happen in his life. For extra impact, he also wrote it out on paper 20 times a day. First he tried positive affirmations to improve his social life. It worked! Soon he was going out on dates, something he had been unable to make happen before. Next, thinking he might want to attend business school, Scott began doing positive affirmations so that he would get a high score on his upcoming entrance exam. He kept affirming that he'd get a score of 94 percent. Sure enough, when the test results arrived in the mail, his grade was 94 percent.

Later he decided he wanted to pursue his dream of being a cartoonist, so he began this daily affirmation: "I will be a successful cartoonist." Sending out samples of his artwork, he got some rejections. However, it wasn't long before a major media company called to sign him up. Soon his cartoon was appearing in some 100 newspapers. Now, Scott Adams and his "Dilbert" cartoon are famous, and he is a millionaire. By the way, he's still doing positive affirmations. When he wrote *The Dilbert Principle* (HarperBusiness, 1996), he affirmed that it would succeed. Sure enough, it rose to the very top of the national best-seller lists.

Chicken Soup success

You've already seen how Mark Victor Hansen and Jack Canfield used visualization to help *Chicken Soup for the Soul* become a best-selling book. Affirmation is another technique they used. Here's how Hansen describes the process:

> We said, if we're going to do a book, let's have a mega-bestseller. Your mind works based on programming, and so what we said is that we'd program each of our minds independently. As we went to sleep, we'd say "Mega best-selling title, mega best-selling title." We'd say it 400 times, because we needed a perfect title for the book...we'd give ourselves a thought command, [saying] "It's going to come to one of us at 4 o'clock." Jack was the blessed one, he woke up, got goosebumps and

said, "Chicken Soup for the Soul!" He called me in the middle of the night and we had the title.

We had the title and went to New York to sell it, and 32 publishers said, "That ain't gonna make it, that's too nicey-nice." Sixty million books later, I think it might make it.

Telling yourself the same positive message over and over again can harness previously untapped power in your mind. Over time, the repeated affirmations recognized by your conscious mind begin to permeate your subconscious. While you do other things or even sleep, your subconscious mind can create imaginative new ways to help manifest the desired result. That's how Jack Canfield was able to summon up such a clever and original title while sound asleep, though some might say he just went to bed hungry! Repeated affirmations can have a powerful effect on your conscious mind, as well. The positive messages help you get an unstoppable belief in your future success. That's why 32 rejections didn't defeat Hansen and Canfield. All those affirmations helped make them true believers in their book and its title, so they stayed the course until the book became a hit.

Your internal conversations

No matter what others say to us, the words that mean the most to us are our internal conversations. This is why self-coaching can be such an effective technique.

At the same time, you must eliminate all negative messages from your internal conversation. Do not ever put yourself down! If you love someone, if you cherish that person so you wouldn't dream of causing him or her pain, you wouldn't ever say something ugly or hurtful or demeaning to that person. In the same spirit, you should never say things to yourself that you wouldn't say to someone you cherish. If you have a pattern of negative self-talk, you know it can defeat your biggest efforts to succeed at almost anything. Now is an excellent time to unlearn this painful habit.

When you say mean-spirited, negative things to yourself, you damage your self-confidence and limit your potential for success. Here are some examples of "never-say" phrases. I want you to read them, add to the list if you want, and then cross them out on this page and never let these words cross your lips again.

- Awful stuff always happens to me.
- I just wasn't meant to succeed.
- I'm such a dummy!
- I can't walk and chew gum at the same time.
- I'm in the way.
- They think I'm stupid.

Before you begin to use positive affirmations, eliminate your negative self-talk. Identify your self-downers and rewrite your internal script now. *Choose to build yourself up, rather than put yourself down.* In the days and weeks ahead, any time you begin telling yourself something negative, *interrupt yourself and clear that thought from your mind.* Do it aloud if you're alone. Say, "Stop. I'm not going to do that any more. I'm a good person." Another way to do this is by taking some physical action. For example, when you catch yourself saying some negative self-talk, snap a rubber band on your wrist to remind yourself how this thinking hurts your progress. But don't turn this into a self-punishment process. You could also stroke your arm to remind yourself to be gentle and kind to yourself. Then immediately replace that negative thought with a strong positive affirmation. Practice this now and see how it feels. Imagine something just went wrong that really upset you. How would you react? If you habitually have a negative thought at these moments, snap a rubber band on your wrist or stroke your arm, then replace that thought with: "From this moment on, today is getting better." Do it whenever you're down, and you can reprogram yourself to feel and act in a positive manner.

Techniques to boost yourself

There are several different ways to explore the path of telling yourself to win. You've read some of the techniques. Perhaps the idea of repeating an affirmation hundreds of times at bedtime, as Jack

Canfield and Mark Victor Hansen did, seems unwieldy to you. If so, there are a variety of other techniques you can try. The important thing to remember about affirmations is that some repetition is necessary to make them work.

Repetition

The most basic way to make affirmations work is to read or repeat a positive affirmation to yourself three times in the morning upon waking, three times at the middle of the day, and again three times before going to bed at night. The more often you read the statement, the better you can see how effectively it's working to help you achieve results. Reading it nine times a day is the absolute minimum. On the other hand, there's no maximum; you really can't say good things to yourself too often. The affirmation only becomes more ingrained the more it's repeated. This is only limited by your time, energy, and level of commitment.

Out loud

Saying the affirmation aloud, with emotion, makes it even more powerful. If you can without disturbing others, say nice things to yourself aloud, with as much feeling as possible. *Really feel* the positive impact and meaning of the words deep within you. If possible, use your body language to emphasize the words.

Eye contact

Try standing before a mirror and looking deep into your own eyes as you affirm. This further impresses the importance of your words on your conscious and subconscious mind.

Written repetition

Another way to add physical impact is to write your affirmations on paper, a minimum of 20 times a day. If your days are spent at a workplace, you might do your midday affirmations in written form, and verbalize the morning and evening sets at home. Also, writing provides visual reinforcement. As mentioned earlier, Scott Adams writes all his affirmations, and he certainly has the success to show for his daily effort.

Flash cards

Copy your affirmations onto several index cards. Put one by your bed and one on your bathroom mirror so you'll be able to read the affirmations first thing each morning and last thing each night. Carry one in your pocket or purse and read it during the day as a pick-me-up. Just pull out the card and tell yourself the positive message again and again to banish defeating thoughts. You can even stick these messages on your car dashboard, on your refrigerator door, or in your personal planner if you have one.

Audio cassette

Record a tape in your own voice, repeating your affirmations over and over again. Listen to the tape while driving your car or while relaxing at home.

Every time you see or hear the message, make a point of saying it a few times aloud or silently. After a while the affirmation will become second nature and you will be able to recite it from memory. While that's a good sign of progress, it's recommended that you keep using the cards or audio cassette, because they provide reinforcement and serve as a physical reminder to keep doing the affirmations.

What to say

Now that you understand how to tell yourself to win, you're nearly ready to explore this path. All you need to do is choose one or more positive affirmations that feel right for you. There are several rules to follow when creating affirmations.

First, always state your affirmations in positive terms, such as, "Money is flowing to me." Avoid using any negative statements, such as "I won't ever be broke again." Negative statements are easily misunderstood by the subconscious mind and you may end up having the reverse of your desires manifest themselves. Speak only in terms of what you want to have happen, never in terms of what you want to avoid.

Second, always state your affirmations in the present tense. If you say, "I *will be* healthy and strong," you're saying you aren't healthy now. Don't use future tense, because it can confuse the subconscious. Instead, say, "I *am* healthy and strong," or even better, "I am getting healthier and stronger every day."

Below are several sample affirmations for specific goals. You can use these or create several original ones. Don't pass up the opportunity to create your own list of affirmations. It's easy and fun, and the positive state of mind it generates is well worth the effort. Besides, putting affirmations in your own words can make them more effective for you.

Wealth creation affirmation: Money is flowing toward me. I grow wealthier and wealthier each day. My success attitude is like a powerful money magnet.

Stop procrastination affirmation: I take positive action to achieve my goals. I get things done! I am free to take action on all my goals.

Positive thinking affirmation: Today is a great day. I look good. I feel successful. I attract success!

Social life/networking affirmation: I enjoy meeting new people. I love listening to others. Each new person that I meet brings me closer to success.

Joy and happiness affirmation: I am full of happiness. I feel joy in being alive. My world is overflowing with happiness. Life gets better and better every day.

Health affirmation: My health gets better and better each day. I feel stronger and healthier than before. My body heals itself. I am a completely healthy person.

Energy affirmation: I feel energized. Power is flowing through me. My energy and enthusiasm bring me complete success!

Stress relief affirmation: I release all my tension. I breathe out all my stress; I breathe in peace and joy. I feel deeply relaxed and completely at peace.

Sales success affirmation: I am confident and sure of success. I like people and they like me. The products I sell help others. I always achieve my highest sales goals!

Now, create your own

The samples above give you a good idea of how to create your own personal messages of success. The advantage of creating your own affirmations is that you can make them as specific as you want. For example, Scott Adams' affirmations are as specific as this: "My book, *The Dilbert Principle*, will become a *New York Times* bestseller."

Obviously, personalized self-coaching phrases are exact and very easy for your mind to absorb and understand. This makes them quite effective. Now it's your turn. Create at least three positive affirmations right now.

My three positive affirmations

1. _____

_____

2. _____

_____

3. _____

_____

Think of these positive statements you just created as advertisements designed to build your self-confidence, get you to your goals, and help you become a success. Tell yourself to win by using these statements today. Repeat the phrases again and again—ideally, with emotion. Like others before you, you may discover that telling yourself to win is your pathway to success.

Today's journal

What mattered to me today:

_____

_____

_____

_____

_____

Coincidences, hunches, breakthroughs I experienced today:

_____

_____

_____

_____

_____

New ideas I had today:

_____

_____

_____

_____

_____

My thoughts, feelings, reflections on today:

_____

_____

_____

_____

_____

Take charge of your life

Goal-setting releases unbelievable power into human personality.

—Dr. Robert Schuller

Welcome back to this journey to success. Your motivation to stay with it has already brought you to the fifth day of the Countdown.

Yesterday, you told yourself to win. Many successful people use daily self-coaching affirmations to get results. Because the positive effects take time to manifest in you, keep using the affirmations daily for the next 17 days. You will know for certain by the end of this time if this technique is part of your personal path to success. If you like the results you're getting, you will want to keep using positive affirmations to accelerate your progress toward success.

Today's concept is *taking charge of your life*. If that phrase resonates with you, maybe your journey to success has had some starts and stops. Maybe at times you felt confident about reaching your dreams, but then those same dreams felt impossibly out of reach. Maybe you are frustrated by how little control you have had over your progress and discouraged by past failures. Before you proceed Day 17, take a few minutes to leave your failures behind you. Take charge of your life by making each day a new beginning and a fresh opportunity.

Don't live in the past

The concept of moving forward has a long and honorable history. In fact, there's an often-quoted Bible passage that underscores the point. In the book of Matthew in the New Testament, Jesus tells a disciple who wanted to stay behind to bury his relative, "Follow me and let the dead bury their dead." In short, he was saying that what lay ahead was more important than what had already been. For our purposes here we might say that, although what happened in the past has value, we need to stop carrying it around like a dead body and simply lay it to rest.

Draw all the knowledge you can from your past experience and then put failures behind you. You can always start anew, regardless of what happened to you in the past. If you're carrying grudges or pain over past incidents, try to resolve those negative feelings with others, and clear them from your heart and mind. If you cannot resolve past hurts or disappointments, then forgive and forget.

No one expects it to be easy to forgive. It is a process of letting go that may need to be done over and over again until you get it right. Forgiving does not mean that the hurt doesn't matter or didn't happen; it means that you do not want to carry it around any longer, so you are laying it down. Also, as long as you carry around the hurt and resentment, you are being hurt by the obsession, while the person who hurt you is not suffering at all. Let go and he or she will have no power over you. You have paid your dues; it is time to take charge of your life and move on.

One way to let go of your stored-up negative thoughts and emotions is to write them all down on paper. Once you have expressed the depth of your feelings in writing, tear up the pages and throw them away, or burn them in the fireplace or on your grill and watch as your past feelings are burned up in the flames, leaving nothing but smoke and ash. This symbolic process can help you let go of the past. Do it and give yourself the freedom and power that comes when you clear away old emotional debris. Take the energy you have wasted on past hurts and put it to work on today. This is a part of taking charge of your life.

Regrets, I've had a few

Along with making each day a new beginning, dismiss any regrets about missed opportunities and focus on the *possibilities of today*. Do not make excuses for what has already happened; just let it go. Apologetic thinking does nothing but limit your outlook and potential. "If only" statements restrict potential for achievement, because they focus on the past and do nothing for the future. Eliminate "if only" statements like the following from your thoughts.

- If only I had started on my goals when I was younger.
- If only I had chosen a career in that field, instead of the one I'm in now.
- If only things hadn't turned out that way.

Remember, it is never too late for great achievement. Consider the following examples.

- Colonel Harlan Sanders launched his Kentucky Fried Chicken food empire when he was in his mid-60s.
- Cecil B. De Mille directed one of the most enduring movies of all time, *The Ten Commandments*, at age 75.
- Virtuoso musician Leopold Stokowsky recorded 20 classical albums when he was in his 90s!

So reset that scoreboard of wins and losses in your mind. Better yet, tear down the scoreboard. Starting today, focus your thoughts on the unlimited potential of today. Banish regrets you have of the past and remove "if only" from your vocabulary. Make every day a new beginning.

If it's going to be, it's up to me

Dr. Robert H. Schuller is a man who believes in the possibilities of today. He calls this "Possibility Thinking." Founder of the Crystal Cathedral in Garden Grove, California, and host of the highly popular *Hour of Power* TV program, Dr. Schuller has written 30 books, consulted with six of the nation's presidents, and at age 70 is still going full speed. His mission is to spread his philosophy of unlimited achievement. His latest book, *If It's Going to Be, It's Up to Me* (HarperCollins, 1997), details the principles of Possibility Thinking. Along with practical ideas, the book is full of rich stories from a lifetime of personal and spiritual success. When I caught up with the tireless Dr. Schuller to ask him about taking charge of one's life, this is what he said:

> *These principles relate to everybody, to the young person who is career-oriented, to the student who's trying to get into the university or post-graduate school. They relate to a husband and wife trying to build a happy relationship. They relate to a teenager who wants to know, "What do I do with my life?" They relate to the man who's retired. They relate to someone who's fighting the battle of cancer.*
>
> *You and you alone are going to decide what your future is going to be. No one else has the power to set your dreams free. If you have a dream, no matter how beautiful but impossible it may be...you are the only one who has the legal authority to write and sign the death sentence to your dream. Don't ever do that! Set your dreams free, don't sentence them to be executed by your negative discouraging thoughts. Set them free, and let them find friends that can help the dreams come true.*

Dr. Schuller agrees that putting failure behind us is important. In school, he was told by a teacher that his writing was poor. Because of that, he put aside his dream of writing. Years later, he was asked to write some articles and saw it as a chance to set his dream free. Sure enough, his articles were so well-regarded, they eventually led him to become a popular author.

The power of goals

There's a classic true story about the power of goals. A top Ivy League school did a research study on its graduating class of 1953. The members of that class were asked if they had a clear, written set of goals for their lives ahead. Only 3 percent had written down their plans and goals for the future. Now let's fast-forward 20 years to 1973. Again the researchers surveyed the members of the class of '53. They discovered that the 3 percent who had started with written goals were worth more financially than the other 97 percent combined! To top it off, the 3 percent seemed happier and more satisfied with their lives than all the other class members.

If results like these sound good to you, then having a set of written goals may be what you need to get moving toward your dreams. However, contrary to what some success books tell you, written goals are not necessary for everyone. I have met a number of very successful people who do not depend on lists of goals to achieve results. People who are excellent at visualizing or who are highly organized often can dispense with writing down their goals. I write down certain daily goals simply because I enjoy the satisfaction of checking them off as I do them. It also keeps me from forgetting to do any of the small ones. When it comes to my long-range goals, I visualize them intently each day. This seems to work for me. Perhaps because writers tend to focus on written words, they naturally favor having written goals. In your case, it's worth exploring this path to see where it leads you. Create a set of written goals for yourself to see if it helps move you forward toward success.

A few days ago, you wrote a lifetime mission for yourself. This mission represents your ultimate lifetime goal. To achieve this long-term goal, you obviously have to achieve a number of short-term goals. This is the list of written goals you will create today. Do not be intimidated by this process; you will be given clear guidelines and many examples of goals to help you decide. But before you begin writing, there is an important point to consider: You must take responsibility for your life.

Be responsible

Written goals can help you take charge of your life, but only if you make the commitment to take complete responsibility for your life as it is. *You alone must be totally responsible for everything that happens to you in every moment.*

For those who prefer blaming others for the poor results in their life, this concept is hard to accept. They would rather say things like:

♦ If my boss wasn't so cheap, I'd be making some real money.

♦ If my parents hadn't given me such low self-esteem, I wouldn't be dating all these jerks.

♦ If those darned kids would just be quiet, I could relax and unwind.

♦ If the government wasn't taxing us to death, we could afford a nice home.

And on and on. Those who put blame and responsibility on anyone and everyone outside their personal circle of control end up feeling like they're not in charge of their lives. They have given away control of their finances, self-esteem, relationships, peace of mind, and life style to outside forces, leaving themselves nothing to do but gripe. And gripe they do, making themselves and everyone around them feel out of sorts.

You have probably heard the saying that you can control no one and nothing but yourself. That means, first, that you *can* control yourself, and second, that no one else can control *you*. It also means that you darn well better control yourself or you will live in a chaotic mess of discontent, because no one else is interested in making your life a bed of roses.

The next step is to take responsibility for everything in your life. Wow! That's a startling and scary idea, but also an empowering step. (Of course, there are acts of nature, like monster storms, and accidents like fires or freeway crashes, that are out of your control. These you can plan for with insurance. While you aren't responsible for them, you are responsible for your attitude, which determines how quickly you recover from them.)

When you stop depending on others to make your life turn out the way you want and realize that you have all the control, you can start to achieve all your goals. Let's look at those gripes again.

- If your boss is underpaying you, you have the power to demand a raise or start looking for a better job.

- If you have low self-esteem, you have the power to build better self-esteem.

- If your kids are noisy and out of control, you have the power to hire a baby sitter, or get them involved in something quiet.

- If your money isn't sufficient for your needs, you have the power to allocate your money differently, learn to live frugally, and even pay less taxes legally.

You get the picture. You have free will. Short of doing something illegal, no one has the right to make you do something you do not want to do. That's why you can take this responsibility for yourself in every area of your life. If you do not, you can be sure someone else will come along and take the control of your life out of your hands. When that happens, your goals can become meaningless.

Another important point: If you don't take responsibility for every outcome in your life, you will probably set limited goals. For example, "Because my parents gave me such low self-esteem, I'd probably be lousy at running a business. I'd love to be an entrepreneur, but I'd better not try that because I'll probably fail." In reality, the only limits on your achievements are the ones you put on them. As Walt Disney said, "If you can dream it, you can do it." Do not limit yourself. Take responsibility for everything that happens to you starting today, and discover unlimited horizons for achievement.

Setting goals

Goal-setting is something that you've probably done many times. For example, taking a drive in the car involves goal-setting. First, you choose a destination. Second, you check a road map, if necessary. Of course, you could just hop in the car, start driving, and hope for the best, but if you don't know how to get there, you will probably have a very hard time reaching your goal. On the other hand, if you have both a clear destination in mind *and* a plan to get there, you have an excellent chance of a successful journey.

Best-selling author Harvey Mackay calls goals "dreams with a deadline." Goal-setting must include a time frame for achievement. Have you considered how long each step on your path toward success will take? As you write your goals, attach deadlines to each of them. The element of time adds motivation and structure to goal-setting.

Break it down

To simplify your goal-setting, I have broken down nearly every possible goal into five distinct groupings: money and abundance, work and career, personal mastery, learning, and inner transformation. You probably have goals in each of these areas. Do not get hung up on the categories, because the goal areas overlap. The point is to make a big task feel easier by breaking it into five steps. Remember, you can change any of your goals anytime you want.

Your ideal life

A few days ago, when you explored the path of visualization, you wrote a description of your ideal future. You may want to refer to that description to help you create a set of written goals. For example, if you imagine living in a different place, then one of yours goals might be to relocate to that new place. If your description of your perfect life includes a different job, then one of your goals might be to take specific action to find that new job.

Money and abundance goals

Let's begin setting goals in the area of money and abundance. These goals include anything involving wealth, acquisition, investments, and retirement. These are fun goals to think about. Start by considering the following samples.

- I want to earn $50,000 a year (or $100,000 or $1 million, etc.). Be specific!
- I want to have a nest egg of (amount) when I retire.
- I want to give money to help others (whom? how much?).
- I want to own a home (where? what size?).

These are just a few examples of money and abundance goals you can consider. Now it's your turn. Write your money and abundance goals right now. Writer John Goddard was naturally a big believer in written goals. He said, "Until you write down your dream, it's just a dream. Writing it makes it a goal." Start writing your goals for the area of money and abundance. Do not worry about editing the list as you write it, just write.

My money and abundance goals

_____

_____

_____

_____

_____

_____

Work and career goals

Next, let's move to the area of work and career. These goals include any that involve work, accomplishment, your business, your job, career, and work achievements. Goals here can bring fulfillment and satisfaction to your life through the expression of your natural skills, talents, and abilities. Consider the following sample work and career goals.

- ♦ I want to start a new career (specify the field).
- ♦ I want a promotion or a new job (be specific).
- ♦ I want to do more to help others through my work (be specific).
- ♦ I want to own a business (doing what?).

These are some examples of work and career goals. Again, it's your turn. Take a few moments now to write out your own goals in this area.

My work and career goals

_____

_____

_____

_____

_____

_____

Personal mastery goals

Now let us determine your personal mastery goals—the positive changes you will make. These might include new and better relationships with friends and loved ones, personal flaws you wish to correct in yourself, personal strengths you wish to develop, healthy habits you wish to establish, mental or emotional changes you wish to make, and so on.

- ♦ I want to lose 20 pounds (or 50 pounds or 100 pounds).
- ♦ I want to have more strength, endurance, and energy.
- ♦ I want to feel more rested and less stressed-out.
- ♦ I want to quit a bad habit (be specific).

These are just some of the goals in this area to consider. Write as many as you wish right now. Don't worry about how impossible to achieve they may seem at this time. Just get the goals in writing.

My personal mastery goals

_____

_____

_____

_____

_____

_____

Learning goals

These are goals concerning the continuing growth, knowledge, and development that is part of every successful life. Here are a few sample learning goals to help you start thinking about your own.

- ♦ I want to earn a degree (specify).
- ♦ I want to learn a foreign language (or learn about another culture, etc.).
- ♦ I want to learn to play a musical instrument (or to act, sing, dance, etc.).
- ♦ I want to learn advanced computer skills.

Write down some goals in the area of learning, knowledge, and education.

My learning goals

_____

_____

_____

_____

_____

_____

Inner transformation goals

Finally, let's move to the area that for some people is the most significant. Inner transformation goals go beyond the basics of everyday life to the deeper beliefs, values, and ideals that bring real meaning and enlightenment to one's existence. Consider the following examples of inner transformation goals.

- ♦ I want to strengthen my belief in (specify).
- ♦ I want to make the world better for others (specify how).
- ♦ I want to build a stronger connection with God.
- ♦ I want to become a more spiritual, giving person.

Take the time to think through your goals of inner transformation. Write all your ideas down now. Do not edit, just jot them down.

My inner transformation goals

_____

_____

_____

_____

_____

_____

Assign deadlines

Now that you have a written set of goals, take a minute to put a deadline for achievement on each one of them. To simplify this process, assume two possible time frames. Some will be short-term goals that you feel are achievable in less than a year. Others will have long-term deadlines, achievable in a year or more. If a goal is realistically achievable in less than a year, write an "S" next to it. If it is a long-term goal, write an "L" next to it. Do this now in the margin next to each of the goals you have listed.

Setting deadlines for your goals creates a structure for your thoughts and a mental framework for accomplishment. The simple act of assigning a deadline to each goal gives your brain a timeline for each goal's completion, and thus begins the process of putting your mind to work turning your goals into reality.

Explore the path of written goals

To see how effective written goals can be in moving you forward, choose several of your most exciting short-term goals to pursue during the rest of the Countdown. By taking daily action on these goals for the next 17 days, you will soon learn whether a written list of goals provides you with the motivating energy you need to make things happen.

Right now, go back and select just three of the most inspiring and exciting short-term goals from your list. Circle the ones you select. For the next 17 days, focus on pursuing these goals. By the way, do not expect to achieve any of these three goals within the next 17 days. Simply pursue each of them actively until the Countdown ends. Go back now, right this minute, and choose three of the most inspiring short-term goals and circle them.

For many people this goal-setting exercise will prove to be one of the more valuable paths to explore. The only way to find out is to try it and see if it works for you. If you have just been reading without involvement, sort of like those people who just stick their toe in the swimming pool instead of jumping in, then now is the time to go back and complete the exercise!

Today's journal

What mattered to me today:

_____

_____

_____

_____

_____

Coincidences, hunches, breakthroughs I experienced today:

_____

_____

_____

_____

New ideas I had today:

_____

_____

_____

_____

My thoughts, feelings, reflections on today:

_____

_____

_____

_____

Simplify everything

It's so easy to get distracted by all the stuff we have in our lives.

—Elaine St. James

Simplicity is a pathway to success? Yes. Although sages through-out history have recommended simplicity as a key to clarity and success, as recently as a decade ago most people would have laughed at the idea. Most modern achievers feel that success has to include a complex life style: Buy the best of everything; have a full, even hectic, social calendar; and spend lots of money pursuing pleasure.

Relatively recently, a significant number of people have rediscovered the wisdom of the sages: Simplicity is the preferred route to freedom, personal power, and peace of mind. (That's *simplicity*, not deprivation.) The clarity they have found, and the lack of emotional, intellectual, and physical clutter they have achieved, has been supported and strengthened by living a concept of simplicity—and that's how they have come to define success. Perhaps your pathway to success includes following a simplified life. Getting rid of external and internal clutter can open doors of insight and opportunity you might otherwise have missed. Uncomplicating your life helps you to focus your energies, accelerating you toward your ultimate goals. Simplicity may or may not be your personal pathway to success, but it is certainly a road worth exploring.

"Travel lightly"

Sonia Choquette, author of *Your Heart's Desire* (Three Rivers Press, 1997), advises that to create the life you want, you must "travel lightly." Yesterday, as part of taking charge of your life, you unburdened yourself of past failures and regrets. Choquette takes us further along this inner path of simplicity by suggesting we not only let go of our concerns, but also discard any narrow opinions and limited views of the world we may hold. Her recommendation is incredibly freeing.

If you cling to the belief that your present view of material and emotional reality is the absolutely correct one, your ability to change the reality of your own existence remains severely limited. Being unable to change your view of the world robs you of the power to change your life for the better. Ask yourself, "If my present view is correct, why isn't my life perfect? What might be holding me back?"

Consider that by letting go of your self-imposed strictures on what is possible and impossible, new vistas of creative opportunity will open for you. Think of the mariners of the ancient world who were convinced that if they sailed too far, they would drop over the edge of the world and be eaten by demons. Today it sounds crazy, but that was reality for those sailors. Are you imposing a similar limit to your quest for success by holding onto your old beliefs? Have you created an edge to your world? Simplify your thinking by opening your mind to new possibilities, and miracles can start to happen for you.

Start with a decision

To introduce simplicity into your life is, well, simple. To begin, all you have to do is agree with yourself to consider the concept. No commitment. No one else needs to know. Just read this chapter, think about it, do the exercises and then, if you choose, make a decision. It's that simple. Nothing has changed at that point but your mind-set: You have decided to consider a different perspective from your current one.

Most of us need a fresh perspective before we can even *consider* letting go of any of our possessions, because we are bombarded daily by messages telling us to buy more. Most of us own more things than we have time or energy to appreciate and enjoy. Yet the prospect of giving up some of our possessions can be intimidating. "Hey! I worked hard for this!" we protest, and we're right. We have endless hours of labor tied up in our possessions. We have exercise equipment that we're too tired to use. There are the pretty things on display that always need dusting. There's the fancy cooking equipment that doesn't get used because we're on a diet because we don't exercise. Perhaps there is the boat that needs a trailer and a slip at the marina, the snowmobile with the broken track, the mountain bike, the RV, the skis, the boxes of stuff we no longer use.... All those toys we purchased to make us feel that we have arrived, that we have accomplished something, that we have created a well-deserved comfortable nest, in reality do little more than complicate our lives.

Interestingly, people who have made the decision to be free of some of the clutter say that it feels like coming out of a stuffy room and drawing in a big breath of fresh air. They say that it doesn't feel like they've lost something. It feels more like they have gained freedom and a sense of lightness.

The simplicity expert

If America has a "simplicity expert," it's probably Elaine St. James. Her decision to follow this path came unexpectedly. After a dozen or so years as an investor, author, and instructor in the real estate field, she was sitting at her desk one day looking at her crowded calendar. Suddenly, she realized the crazy schedule wasn't fun anymore. Her life had become far too complicated, and it was insane trying to jam all this stuff into her every waking moment. At that instant, she made a decision: She was going to simplify.

She began creating a list of things she could eliminate from her life. Luckily, her husband agreed with her plan, and they started a life-changing process of simplification. First, she canceled call waiting on the telephone. Next, she cut back on magazine subscriptions, eliminating those that piled up unread on the table. She eliminated several credit cards, thereby reducing the monthly mail. The couple streamlined their home care and lawn care by making changes in their routine and layout. The list of things to simplify soon totaled more than 80 items. That simplification plan eventually turned into St. James's first book on the subject, *Simplify Your Life* (Hyperion, 1994). Since then, she's written two more books, *Inner Simplicity* (Hyperion, 1995) and *Living the Simple Life* (Hyperion, 1996), and has become a nationally recognized authority on the subject. Here's what St. James told me about the growing interest in simplification.

> *Our lives have gotten too complicated. Never before in the history of the world have so many of us been able to have so many things. We've been led in recent years to believe that we can have them all, and we've worn ourselves out trying. Many people feel that lack of connection with their creativity because they're distracted by all these things.*

How many activities do you feel compelled to do each day because you're accustomed to the pattern of your life? Chances are, if you dropped them from your ritual, you wouldn't miss them. Have comfortable habits and routines trapped you into wasting time and energy on a daily basis? St. James told me:

> *Habit is what keeps us doing all these routine things. We're afraid that if we don't do it all we're going to miss something. I finally realized that, yes, I'm going to miss something, but that that would be okay, I'll survive. Not only survive, but thrive, because I'm not trying to do it all.*
>
> *Look at some of the people who've made major contributions to the world of art, music, or science. Picasso, Mozart, Einstein—these people led pretty simple lives. They focused on their main area, tapped their creative inner source, and had rich, wonderful lives.*

Getting rid of a lot of stuff and not allowing ourselves to go out and acquire more can free up a lot of time and energy for the things we really want to do.

Saving time

Saving time isn't a small matter. Each day has only 24 hours. Every minute wasted is gone forever. Those wasted minutes add up to time you could have used to reach the success that would fulfill your life's purpose. A recent survey showed that six out of 10 people found life more hurried today than it was five years ago. Life is more rushed than it was a generation ago, yet each hour today contains the same number of minutes it always has. We're just trying to jam more into the days, and it's creating stress and complications. Streamlining your life, getting rid of the intellectual and physical clutter, is the best solution. You will feel like you have more time and you will enjoy your time more.

Making the decision to simplify your life begins with the process of clearing away what does not matter so you can focus your energies on what does matter. Simplifying your life soon becomes an ongoing process as you discern new areas that you want to clean up. The energy and time you gain from losing the clutter will contribute to your health, sense of well-being, important relationships, and the successful accomplishment of your goals.

Living space

At one time I lived in a two-bedroom apartment that was filled with furnishings, books, tapes, magazines, plants, artwork, computer equipment, stereo gear, and all sorts of other possessions. It had lots of large windows, but it always felt cramped. After a few years, I decided to move to a larger place. Over a period of weeks I packed and shipped off many boxes of nonessentials to the new place. As this went on, I noticed that the character of my apartment began to change. The added open space felt extremely pleasant. Removing the clutter was like turning down an irritating noise. It was both calming and energizing, and my daily life was easier. Whatever I needed was always right at hand. Distractions were minimized, time was saved, even cleaning was simpler and faster.

That was a great lesson for me. I have since given away many things that I once thought I needed, and tossed out other stuff. My living space today is as simple as possible and this keeps me focused on what matters most to me. Periodically, I still have to go through and get rid of the accumulation that seems to multiply on its own. Every time I do it, it seems to provide me with a fresh burst of energy to achieve more.

The 3,000-year-old practice of *feng shui,* the Chinese art of place-ment, explains this phenomenon. Feng shui, a Far Eastern technique to organize work and home space for optimum results, is gaining popularity in the West. It is a method that maximizes energy flow, or *chi,* by proper placement and organization of every room. Those who advocate feng shui begin with the key principle of getting rid of clut-ter, which is believed to release blocked energy in everything from your work to your health. As you can see, the idea of simplifying your life to maximize your sense of well-being is not a new one.

Where to start

Simplifying your life is easiest when it's done gradually. Start by making a list of some areas of your life that need to be simplified. Break it down into these categories: objects, tasks, papers, money.

Objects. Clean out your wardrobe by giving clothes you don't wear to charity. Clean off shelves, cupboards, and drawers jammed with items rarely used. (If you can't decide what to keep, a good rule of thumb is, if you haven't used it in a year, out it goes. Generally these objects contribute little or nothing to the quality of your life.)

Tasks. Limit your shopping to one day a week and do all your regular errands in a single trip. Make household chores easier by re-arranging furniture to allow for quicker cleaning. Organize your bill paying, banking, and telephone calls more efficiently.

Papers. This is an area that trips up many of us. Dump the stacks of magazines and newspapers that have piled up. If they con-tain articles you want, tear out the articles and toss the rest. Organize correspondence and paperwork. When possible, do it immediately. (A recent survey showed that people can spend as much as four hours a week searching for misplaced paperwork!) Cancel subscriptions that mean little to you. Donate books you have read to the local library.

Money. Review the services you pay for, like telephone and cable TV, to see what's necessary and what's complicating your life. Set up automatic payroll deposit and savings plans to avoid wasting time on these each month. Consolidate your investments, and limit your bank accounts and credit cards to the minimum.

Now it's your turn. Write down a list of ways in which you can simplify your life.

Ways to simplify my life

_____

_____

_____

_____

_____

_____

_____

_____

Now that you have listed some areas for simplification, put the plan into action. Clearing away years of accumulated clutter and habit-bound activity is not an overnight project. Take it one step at a time, but be sure to employ what I call the *domino process*. Make the first simplification project you tackle a very visible one. For example, clear off a shelf that you see every day, one that's in plain view. That highly visible shelf will look so great to you when it's clutter-free, it will inspire you to take another step in the same way that the first domino in a row knocks down the second one. Make your second project another one you will really notice. That visible success will encourage you to simplify something else. Soon your gratification will have you simplifying everything in all parts of your life.

"The big issues"

Once you have all this additional time, what do you do with it? During a radio interview, Elaine St. James shared with me what she did. She put it to work on some of the big issues in her life that were troubling but that she had never before had time to resolve:

> *My big issue had been anger. I'd developed the habit as a child of reacting to situations with anger, but I'd never taken the time to stop and look at why I did it and how it complicated my life. Once I took the time I was able to deal with this issue. That step helped me free up even more time and energy.*
>
> *Saying you don't have the time is a great excuse that keeps you from exploring your big issues. Perhaps the relationship you're involved in isn't working, or you're having problems with the kids, or you don't like your job. Simplifying your life gives you the time to look at those issues, and make the changes you need to make so you can create a wonderful life.*

Taking the simplified path to success can reveal hidden clues to a more fulfilling life. Have you ever lost a small object on your desk or kitchen table? After moving stuff around, searching under and between things with no luck, most people begin clearing the junk away to help them locate the missing item. When the desk or table is cleared of clutter, the hidden object becomes visible. In the same way, simplifying your physical surroundings, your obligations, your activities, and your thinking can make important hidden issues visible, and even reveal the doorway to your ultimate goals.

In the words of Henry David Thoreau, "Simplify, simplify." His move to the solitude of Walden Pond gave him the clarity of mind to sort through personal issues. Explore the path of a simplified life starting today, and discover if it leads you to the fulfillment, peace of mind, and success you've been seeking.

Today's journal

What mattered to me today:

_____

_____

_____

_____

_____

Coincidences, hunches, breakthroughs I experienced today:

_____

_____

_____

_____

New ideas I had today:

_____

_____

_____

_____

My thoughts, feelings, reflections on today:

_____

_____

_____

_____

Celebrate and reflect

No one can tell you you're successful. It comes only from within.

—Gerard Smith

Today, your seventh day in the Countdown, is a change of pace in *Countdown to Success*. According to Biblical tradition, the seventh day is when God rested after creating the Earth. Whether you are a spiritual person, an atheist, or somewhere in between, you probably recognize the value in taking time periodically to pause and reflect before moving on. Just as your body requires regular rest periods for optimum performance, so do your mind and spirit. This is a time when lessons of a higher nature can be considered and we can seek out the true meaning of our lives. So today, let us heed the ancient counsel that tells us the seventh day is a special one.

Behind the tradition

From a religious standpoint, the seventh day of rest is observed widely. In the Christian tradition, the Sabbath day is Sunday. In

Jewish tradition, Saturday is observed as the Sabbath (as it is for a few Christian groups, including Seventh Day Adventists). The word Sabbath comes from the Hebrew *shavat*, which means to cease, desist, or rest. Today, you will take a mini-sabbatical from this 21-day process of self-discovery.

A day of meaning

This day is a point in the Countdown to reflect on the meaning of success. While you enjoy the change of pace today, spend some time celebrating the successes you have already achieved. There's a saying: Success is a journey, not a destination. There's a bit of joy within each step of that journey.

Your life can be a very positive experience every single day. I am not being a Pollyanna; I am being realistic. You get to decide how to see your world. Even the worst failures and most negative experiences carry valuable lessons. Each failure brings you closer to success. If you can learn to appreciate all things in your life today, both good and bad, you make your daily existence more fulfilling. That attitude can inspire you to greater achievement. Success isn't something you have to wait for, something that comes only in the future; it's something you can enjoy a bit of right now by appreciating the small successes along the way, every day. Adopt this attitude now. Allow yourself to feel that you are already a success in many ways. It can make your journey on whatever path you choose more meaningful, and it can move you closer to your ultimate goals.

Harold Kushner has written a number of inspiring books. One of them, *When All You Ever Wanted Is Not Enough* (Pocket Books, 1986), examines the meaning of life. We are all driven to achieve, he says, to show everybody what we are capable of doing. Unfortunately, this sometimes takes up our entire lives. We never take time to make meaningful connections with the people in our lives, figuring there will always be time to get around to that later. We put off connecting with our loved ones, or with the beautiful moments of life each day, until it is too late. On our deathbed, we never say, "I wish I'd spent more time on business," Kushner profoundly observes.

Start to experience the things in life that really count, beginning today. Do you think there's not much that's great about your life right now? Do you believe that it is not possible for your life to be a positive experience every single day? Let's test that point of view with a little exercise. Write down five things—only five things—that you find worth celebrating right now. Imagine that I am standing in front of you with a bottle of champagne and two glasses, and I want to celebrate something with you. If you don't drink alcohol, then imagine that it's something you would enjoy using to make a toast. What would you make a toast to?

Here are some ideas to get your mind working:

- Celebrate the basic fact that you have life and health.

- Celebrate the love of your friends and family.

- Celebrate that you have a good mind and that you're capable of learning something new each day.

- Celebrate the progress you've made toward success.

- Celebrate that you're living in an exciting time in history when there are new discoveries, technologies, and ideas.

Do you have five things to write down yet? Now think of five more. When you realize all you can celebrate right now, you realize also that there are positive happenings in your life every day. A positive outlook is just as realistic as a pessimistic one, yet it gives you far more enthusiasm and energy to reach your goals than a negative point of view does.

10 things worth celebrating right now

1. _____

2. _____

3. _____

4. _____

5. _____

6. _____

7. _____

8. _____

9. _____

10. _____

Take the time to celebrate the good things, to connect with those you love, and to "high five" your triumphs *every* day. Today will only happen once and then it is gone forever. Okay, at the end of some days we are inclined to sigh and say, thank goodness that's over. But, if we made it through, we are stronger and smarter for what we learned. So appreciate each day, and recognize what a wonderful miracle it is to be alive and breathing and working toward your goals.

Life-changing experiences

Some of us begin to appreciate life only after nearly losing it. Dannion Brinkley, author of *Saved by the Light* (HarperCollins, 1994), and Betty J. Eadie, author of *Embraced by the Light* (Gold Leaf Press, 1992), were both profoundly changed for the better by their near-death experiences (NDEs). Many people have been changed by NDEs.

One afternoon an average guy was repairing his pickup truck. The jack slipped and the vehicle fell onto his chest. By the time an emergency team arrived, his heart had stopped and he wasn't breathing. At the hospital, to the astonishment of the doctors, the man suddenly began breathing again and soon he revived completely. Now, fully recovered from his accident, he is a changed man. He says his NDE gave him a glimpse of the afterlife and changed his outlook on life dramatically. Now he appreciates things he once took for granted, like his children, his family, and simple pleasures. Now meaningful conversations and helping others are what is most important to him. He says he is much happier than before, more at peace with himself, and he enjoys life as much as possible every day.

A profound secret of success

This man in the preceding true story has apparently discovered the profound secret of how to achieve happiness: to appreciate the gift of life, to enjoy life every day, and to make life better for others. As formulas go, this is a great one for success. Most people think that good feelings have to come from outside and they seek fulfillment through others' good opinions of them, from pleasurable or ego-boosting situations, or even from substances such as drugs and alcohol. Through the ages people have acquired wealth and luxury, yet have failed to capture a feeling of true happiness or fulfillment, because they never discovered the profound secret of how to do so.

Celebrating success

In *Celebrating Success* (Health Communications, 1997), Gerard Smith has put together a fascinating collection of letters from kings, movie stars, athletes, entrepreneurs, and many other highly regarded people, giving their definitions of success. Recently Smith told me that not one person defined success in terms of financial wealth! Instead, they told about such things as happiness, service to others, inner growth, personal responsibility, reaching for goals, and giving back to the world. Is it a coincidence that all of these wealthy and famous people define success in these terms? Of course not! They view success according to *how they live*, not in terms of wealth or renown, which is a big reason why they became so successful in the first place.

Regardless of the difficulties, pressures, or stresses that you feel as you pursue your goals, take the time to value what is good in your life every day. Celebrate the little triumphs as well as the big ones. Happiness and fulfillment are self-generated feelings. You get them from daily appreciation and connection with the people and events in your life.

No limits

How is your attitude toward success? Do you feel limited or insufficient? Feelings like that can hold back your progress toward goals because they make you feel incomplete. Adopt the unlimited attitude of those who know they are complete within themselves, and therefore need nothing outside of themselves to feel complete and whole. Achieving success flows naturally from this knowing, because it is a position of strength and self-assurance. On the other hand, if you think you are limited, your results will usually be limited too.

In his book *Your Sacred Self* (HarperCollins, 1995), Dr. Wayne W. Dyer describes this changed perspective as moving from *striving* to *arriving*. It's common to hear people come up with all sorts of reasons for feeling unsuccessful. Of course, it is a lot easier to make excuses than to change one's attitude. How limited is your perspective? These two stories may alter how you see your apparent limitations, as they did for me.

Chris Klein of Lombard, Illinois, has a form of cerebral palsy that severely damaged the brain regions controlling his muscles. According to the *Chicago Tribune*, he can't talk, write, walk, dress himself, or feed himself. He can control only his left foot, so he uses the toes of that foot to type on a special keyboard to communicate. Early in life, several school teachers told him to forget any plans for higher education. Despite his apparent limitations and the discouragement from others, he graduated with a specialized degree from Hope College in Holland, Michigan. Currently, he's pursuing his master's degree in Divinity. He told the newspaper reporter who interviewed him that he considers his body a gift from God, meant to encourage others who believe they are limited by disability.

French magazine editor Jean-Dominique Bauby had every excuse to feel limited. After suffering a massive stroke, he was almost fully paralyzed and speechless. Yet his mind was unaffected, and his ability to create and reason was unimpaired. After wasting many days feeling sorry for himself, he decided not to let physical limitations hold him back and to fulfill his dream of writing a book. With supreme effort, he learned to communicate by rapidly blinking one eye, which was the only part of his body still under his control. Incredibly, he created a unique kind of code to spell words one by one. Assisted by a friend, he began dictating his book, *The Diving Bell and the Butterfly* (Knopf, 1997), one letter at a time. It's estimated that Bauby had to blink his eye several hundred thousand times as he spelled out words one by one for his book of more than 100 pages. Though Jean-Dominique Bauby recently passed away, his book won the praise of critics and became a bestseller in France.

Once you refuse to make excuses or recognize limitations, it's incredible what you can achieve. Do you still feel limited after reading about Klein and Bauby? Or do you realize just how successful and complete you already are? With this realization, you have gone from striving to arriving. Your new-found attitude enables you to achieve anything you desire.

The power within you

A king in a distant land had heard of Moses, the prophet and lawgiver, but had never met him. The ruler was curious, so he asked his astrologers to study their charts and tell him what kind of man Moses was. The astrologers looked at their mystic symbols and told the king that Moses was a mean, deceitful, hateful man, with many vices and weaknesses. This surprised the king, because he had heard such good things about Moses. Years later, the ruler finally did meet Moses, and found him a wise and caring man. He told Moses of how his astrologers had described him. Moses replied, "Your astrologers were right. They described the person that I was once, the person I had to conquer, so that I could become the person I am today."

Moses understood what most people deny: that each of us has the power within to overcome all of our apparent limitations. It is easy to place the blame on our flaws, upbringing, circumstances, fate, bad luck, poor timing, etc. Placing blame outside ourselves provides easy excuses for not changing. When we accept ourselves and take responsibility for the way we are, we take command of our power to achieve. This power is within each of us, just waiting to be released.

Some people assume they will raise their personal standards, lose their bad habits, and improve everything about themselves when they become successful. They have missed the point! By not making these changes in themselves today, they accept mediocrity, and that holds them back from higher achievement. The changes do not happen instantly; success comes in a series of small advances, day by day, that in time reward us with our ultimate goals.

This marks your completion of the first third of *Countdown to Success*. As I said in the Introduction, I hope you planned a personal celebration for today to reward yourself for your progress. Make this an even bigger event by celebrating all that is great in your life. Celebrate the successes you have achieved already. Adopt the attitude of being a complete and whole person, as you are, and refuse to let anything hold you back from the success you deserve.

Today's journal

What mattered to me today:

_____

_____

_____

_____

_____

Coincidences, hunches, breakthroughs I experienced today:

_____

_____

_____

_____

New ideas I had today:

_____

_____

_____

_____

My thoughts, feelings, reflections on today:

_____

_____

_____

_____

Face your fears

At the bottom of all our fears is simply the fear that we can't handle what life hands us.

—Susan Jeffers

You're entering the middle third of the Countdown. Have any of the different paths resonated with you? Stay alert for any of the coincidental or intuitive experiences signaling that you are moving in the right direction. There are more paths ahead for you to test, but no journey of value is made without encountering some obstacles along the way. When you are finally moving along your perfect path to success, those obstacles can pop up and stop you dead in your tracks if you don't have ways to handle them. So for the next few days, let us take a break in exploring new paths and learn ways to master four of the most common obstacles to success.

The Failure Four

Achievers I have researched and interviewed have revealed that there are four invisible, internal, and basic obstacles to success. These are states of mind that I call the *Failure Four*. (No, that's not the name of an alternative rock group!) The Failure Four are destructive patterns of thought.

The Failure Four

1. Fear and worry.
2. Lack of confidence.
3. Lack of persistence.
4. Failure to take action.

If these four seem familiar, it is because they are common obstacles faced by most people on the path to success. But every successful person has learned to master these challenges, and you can, too. Because each of the Failure Four is a pattern of thought, over the next four days you will overcome these challenges by creating a new state of mind about each pattern. To help you make these changes, you will employ visualization, mental imagery, and written exercises.

FRANK AND ERNEST reprinted by permission of Newspaper Enterprise Association, Inc.

Defining fear and worry

Today let's examine two things that keep many people from moving forward and achieving success. The first is fear, and the second is worry. Fear is a powerful emotion that can accompany any transition, any new experience, or any unknown or dangerous situation. Fear can be strong and immediate, such as what you might experience if you were confronted by a lion. Fear can stop you dead in your tracks and paralyze you when you most need to take action. (Of course, fear in some situations helps you stay alive. For example, a fear of heights might keep you from taking a risky stroll along the edge of a high cliff. But in this chapter, we look at unproductive fears that keep you from achieving results you really desire.)

Fear is felt by almost everyone from time to time. Mastering fear means learning how to deal with it. Susan Jeffers, Ph.D., is the author of the classic bestseller, *Feel the Fear and Do It Anyway* (Fawcett Books, 1987), which has sold in 22 countries. Her explanation of the meaning of fear sums it up perfectly. Jeffers says, "At the bottom of all our fears is simply the fear that we can't handle what life hands us."

Worry, on the other hand, is generally a troubling, uneasy feeling. There is also a time difference between fear and worry. While fear is often felt in the here and now, worry is almost always about some future situation. Worry is not as bad as the gut-wrenching anxiety or dread that fear causes, but worry can make you waste time, lose sleep, accumulate physical damage, feel stressed out, and rob you of the personal power you need for achievement.

To further clarify the distinction between fear and worry, think of fear as *acute* emotion and worry as *chronic* emotion. By the way, do not confuse worry with being concerned and caring, as in, "I was so worried about you." Worry is nothing more than chronic negative thought, far different from the positive states of concern and caring for others.

Feeling the fear

The title of Susan Jeffers' book is also the message: *Feel the Fear and Do It Anyway*. Jeffers explained to me that the ultimate way to feel the fear and do it anyway is to access the power of your *higher self*. Susan Jeffers says:

> *Most of us live in the world of the lower self, that could be defined by the chatterbox, that little voice inside that tries to pull us down with "What if?* *and "Should I?"* *and drives us*

crazy. When we learn how to access the highest part of who we are, then we're at peace.

The process of getting to this higher place within you is an ongoing process, what Jeffers calls "a lifelong journey," and which she discusses as a spiritual process in her book, *End the Struggle and Dance With Life* (St. Martin's Press, 1996). You needn't be actively religious, but it helps to recognize the existence of a higher power—call it God, Spirit, the Universe, or whatever you prefer—and to realize that a part of this universal power and intelligence exists within you. This part is your higher self.

Accessing your higher self on a daily basis will eventually dissolve your fears. You will begin to see that because the same force that created you also created the rest of the universe, fear is unnecessary. You will begin to feel guidance and support that transcend your fears. This isn't just an intellectual belief, but an absolute inner conviction. The best way to access your higher self is through meditation. We will explore the concept of the higher self and meditation in later chapters. For now, just have faith that this is the ultimate tool you can use to master all negative emotions, including fear.

Faith beats fear

Faith itself is a powerful force to dissolve fear. Consider the counsel of Joe Tye, author of six books including *Never Fear, Never Quit* (Delacorte Press, 1997). Tye has made it his life mission to teach self-empowerment to others, and he organizes programs to do that, including an annual Never Fear, Never Quit conference. Some time ago, Joe Tye sent me a small card containing the following words:

- Fear is a reaction, courage is a decision.
- Fear is a coward, it only attacks when you are weak and confused.
- Fear is many tomorrows, courage is one today.
- Fear creates enemies, courage creates friends.

♦ Give fear a name and it becomes just a problem.

♦ With faith, fear becomes an ally.

As these statements reveal so clearly, dissolving fear becomes possible when you simply change the way you think about it. At the moment you feel fear, the most important thing to have is faith that you will survive that circumstance; not only survive, but become stronger, wiser, and a far better person from that particular experience. Let's say you are very afraid of walking out on stage to give a speech, but you have faith that a higher power put you in this situation for a reason, and that power is not about to let you fail. Your faith helps get you through the speech. After the speech is done, you have no more fear of it—and you discover how much you have learned from the challenging experience.

You may be fearful about asking your boss for a raise or a promotion, but you have the faith that everything will be fine, no matter what the boss's reaction. After you have talked to the boss, your fear of asking the question is gone—and you have a much clearer picture of where you stand at work. Depending on the answer you receive from the boss, you might suddenly improve your present salary or position, or find you have the courage to seek out a more lucrative job elsewhere. Burning faith in a positive outcome, no matter what may happen in the short term, will melt away your fears like a blazing flame melts ice.

In past chapters we've discussed a number of tools to help you get past your fears. The first is to take responsibility for yourself in every way. This puts you fully in charge of your destiny. It empowers you. No longer do you let others' opinions or fears affect you, because you are in charge of how you feel. You don't accept others' limits. If your fears come from someone else's limiting beliefs, taking responsibility for your own beliefs lets you release those old fears. For example, you may says things like, "I just know I'll make the wrong decision. My husband says I have lousy instincts." Or "My mother always warns me to be careful. If I blow this I'll never hear the end of it." In these cases, your fear stems from what other people think. Take charge of your own feelings and toss out the fear.

A second tool we have already discussed is recognizing the positive qualities of your life every day. Feeling good about yourself and your life tends to banish fear. A constant flow of positive thoughts and feelings naturally dissolves negative thinking. Writing down all the positive results that will come from pushing through your fears is a wonderful thing to do. It helps you develop the faith that there are good things ahead, and fear fades.

A third tool we have considered is self-coaching affirmations. You've probably used them already. "C'mon, I can do it.... Everything's gonna be okay.... Steady now, here I go!" When you really want to do something, these affirmations rise automatically. But you don't have to wait for them. Start assuring yourself that you will master your fears and then watch how fast you progress.

Finally, because fear is such a strong emotion it can affect you physically. The common symptoms of fear include tense muscles, a dry mouth, pounding heart, and fast, shallow breathing. Take control when you feel your body reacting to fear. Inhale slowly and deeply, hold for a few seconds, and then slowly exhale while you visualize your fears departing with your exhaled breath. Repeat this exercise for several minutes and notice how your symptoms of fear recede. If possible, retreat to a quiet place and close your eyes. Intently picture a positive outcome while you do the breathing exercise.

Conquer worry

Worry is less destructive and limiting than fear, and it can be dealt with in simpler ways. (However, worry can lead to fear if we let it become obsessive worry.) Realize also that many of the techniques you use to beat worry can also be used to *weaken* your fears.

Grab a pencil or pen and let's jump into today's exercise. You are going to write down five things you have worried about recently. If you own your own business, maybe you've been worried about where it's going and what the future holds. If you work for a company, perhaps you've been worried about your job and whether you will be laid off or fired. Maybe you're looking for a job and you are worried that you won't be able to find one. If you're a student, maybe schoolwork is causing worry. Or perhaps you are worried about your health.

You may have worries about your weight or your appearance. Perhaps your relationships, your marriage, or your family are making you worry. Maybe you have been worrying about things you have been putting off, such as making a career move. Money and finances often cause worry. And some people worry about global issues, such as the environment, the economy, or a current crisis. Whatever your worries are, go ahead and write down five of your most recent ones.

5 worries I have experienced recently

1. _____

2. _____

3. _____

4. _____

5. _____

Meaningless worry

You will have to learn to take away the power these worries have over you. By visualizing the outcomes of your worries and putting them in writing, you will gain perspective and therefore control over worry.

First, let's see if there are any *meaningless worries* on your list, things beyond your control. Calling them meaningless does not mean they are unimportant; in fact, they can be extremely important, but the clue to knowing if they're meaningless is whether you can solve the problem on your own. If you cannot, then it's important not to let it intrude on your thoughts in the way that issues do that you *can* change. For example, can you affect the nation's economy personally or stop the threat of nuclear war on your very own? Probably not. Then the economy and nuclear war are meaningless worries until you are in a position to change them. They are issues that are okay to be concerned about, but not worth your worry. If you work for a large company, can you really control whether you will be laid off? If not, then that's a meaningless worry. If any of your worries are meaningless, realize that spending time worrying about them is a waste of your time and energy. When a worry starts bothering you, first ask yourself if the outcome is beyond your control. If so, worrying won't make any difference, so relax and let go of your meaningless worries.

The business and the baby

A woman I interviewed recently shared with me a story about her past meaningless worries. It was the early 1950s, and two dates on her calendar had her in a total frenzy. On September 1, a small mail-order ad she had placed was to appear in *Seventeen* magazine to launch her new business. As any budding entrepreneur knows, it's easy to worry when you are starting a business. On February 3, her first baby was due. There was no reason for her to worry, because all the signs were positive in both cases. She'd done her homework on the magazine ad, and her health and the doctor's reports on the baby were fine. Nevertheless, she obsessed for weeks, and it did nothing but exhaust her at a time when she needed the energy most. These qualify as meaningless worries.

Looking back, she realizes how foolish her worries were. Her ad for monogrammed belts and purses was a huge success and she got thousands of orders. Her baby was born healthy a few months later. This elegant and successful woman is Lillian Vernon, founder of the Lillian Vernon Corporation. Today she's one of the world's most successful women entrepreneurs and she has put all her worries behind her.

Don't let meaningless worries hold you back or wear you down. If worrying about something won't make any difference, let go of it.

Visual perspective

The next step to controlling worry is to gain perspective on your worries, by *visualizing and comparing outcomes*. Everyone has concerns. Worriers tend to blow those concerns out of proportion by imagining the worst. To gain visual perspective and control worry, first visualize and write down the *worst possible outcome*, followed by a more *realistic outcome.*

Consider the five worries you have listed on page 96. Imagine their worst possible outcomes. What is the worst thing that could happen in each case? For example, if you are worried about a plane flight you will soon be taking, your worst outcome might be that the plane will crash. If you are worried about problems at work, your worst outcome might be that you will get fired. Those are serious worst-case scenarios! But it's not uncommon for worriers to imagine the worst happening to them. Write down the worst possible outcomes of your five worries.

The five worst possible outcomes

1. _____
2. _____
3. _____
4. _____
5. _____

The final step in this process is to contrast those worst-case scenarios with more realistic outcomes. Psychologists treating severe worriers sometimes use a similar technique, called Cognitive Therapy. Question your five worst-case assumptions. Really interrogate yourself! What are the actual odds that something that disastrous could really happen? Get an accurate view of the situation. If you're not exactly sure of the facts, check things out and get answers. To use my previous example, if you are worried about safety during an upcoming plane trip, what are the actual odds of a crash occurring? By knowing the facts, you'll be able to confidently visualize a safe arrival at your destination and get control over your worry. The fact is, major airlines in the U.S. have only four or five fatal accidents a year, out of about seven million annual departures! As you can see, this worry is not based on realistic odds of disaster occurring.

Knowing the facts can give you perspective and therefore control over worry. Let's look at another example. If you have an ongoing problem at work, picture what might *realistically* happen. Be realistic and visualize the situation objectively. Then write down five *realistic outcomes* to your worries. Again, this might require a little investigation and checking of facts on your part. You might want to talk to a few people who have faced similar worries. You could look up the odds of a worst-case outcome. Do whatever it takes to transform your mental picture of the outcome into something much more realistic, and write these realistic outcomes down now.

5 realistic outcomes of my five worries

1. _____

2. _____

3. _____

4. _____

5. _____

Control those worries!

Most people who worry never gain perspective on their fears. Instead, they get caught up in their worries and obsess endlessly. In fact, some people are worried that if they stop worrying, something even worse will happen! But as you've learned, chronic worry is basically a problem of perspective. Get the right perspective on a situation, and the worry is minimized and controlled.

If worry sometimes limits your progress, keep a pad of paper handy for the next 14 days. Whenever a worry pops into your mind, write it down along with your visualization of the worst possible outcome. Then dig into it, get the facts, and visualize the realistic outcome to get a true perspective on your worries. Do this for two weeks and you will strengthen your ability to control worry. Also, you can gain perspective by talking through your worries with friends and family. But avoid people who tend to magnify your worries. Talk through your worries only with people who have a realistic, positive outlook on life.

A time for worry

A final way to control your worry is to set a time each week to devote yourself completely to worrying about whatever is bothering you. Anytime a worry starts to intrude on your thoughts during the week, simply put it off and add it to your list of worries to think about during your regular weekly worry-time.

A very creative fellow was constantly working on new projects and always tackling new challenges. At times, money was tight. Investors wanted to see results, not promises. So, this man had a lot to worry about. While working on Project A, he would find himself distracted by a sudden worry: Was Project B going well? Were his assistants following through? Finally, this creative man decided to work out a system to manage his worry. He would devote exactly one hour every Friday afternoon to do nothing but worry. Anytime a worry would pop into his head and distract him, he would simply jot it on the list he used to keep track of worries. Then each Friday, for one hour, he would review his list. That very creative man was Thomas Edison. Edison noticed that by the time Friday rolled around, the worries on his list were often no longer significant or meaningful. As the inventor discovered, scheduling a set period of time to handle worry is an efficient way to manage it.

Whatever method you choose to manage and master your fears and worries, follow through and learn to overcome these common challenges to success. Refuse to let negative thoughts stop your progress on your chosen path to success.

Today's journal

What mattered to me today:

_____

_____

_____

_____

_____

Coincidences, hunches, breakthroughs I experienced today:

_____

_____

_____

_____

New ideas I had today:

_____

_____

_____

_____

My thoughts, feelings, reflections on today:

_____

_____

_____

_____

Take risks with confidence

We can learn to be more confident, but first we've got to understand what confidence is: Confidence is an attitude.

—Walter Anderson

Lack of confidence is a common deterrent to success that you can overcome. By the way, swaggering egotism and cockiness aren't confidence. Real confidence is an *inner knowing* that you are okay with taking risks. Why is this inner knowing so important? Because any really significant movement along the path to success will involve risk, and because you may face your greatest risks early in your quest for success.

On the way to any major goal there comes at least one point of no return, and at that jumping-off place you must be ready for risk. You have to be willing to accept risk to keep moving forward. If the risk makes you stop, your advancement will stop. To cross such chasms of risk successfully, you must plan for risk before you face it.

The kinds of risk

Walter Anderson is author of *The Confidence Course* (Harper-Collins, 1997), a book based on the popular course he teaches at the New School in New York. In a recent radio interview, he explained to me that there are three kinds of losses we face in taking a risk:

The first is a positive loss. We recognize that we're not happy about something.... For example, "Gee I don't really like this job," or "I don't like where I live." Once we say that, we don't deny that any longer, and we have to do something about it.

Second is practical loss, what you give up to take the risk to go ahead. For example, to go from one job to another, you're giving up the job you have. Or to break up a relationship, you're giving up the partner you have.

Third is the potential loss. It's what happens when the risk doesn't work out the way you wanted. What do you lose? You know, we spend a lot of time on that, and the truth is that's not what stops us from taking the risk. What stops most of us from taking risks is the practical loss, what we have to give up to get ahead. Like the soldier in a war, we'll struggle so much harder to hold on to what we have than to get something new.

Nearly anyone who has achieved great prosperity, great personal fulfillment, or great success of any kind can tell you about a personal test of courage they faced along the way. For those who have successfully followed their path to achieve their destiny, the point of no return came the moment they gave up something to move ahead. For many, it is a job they had to leave. But a more common scenario goes something like this:

Richard's job provides him an income, yet he dreams constantly of owning his own business. He knows he faces a financial risk in pursuing this dream. Can he afford to quit his job to take a chance on future success? Others warn him not to think about it because the risk appears insurmountable. Rather than develop a careful plan to help him face this risk confidently, Richard chooses to do nothing at all. Not surprisingly, his dream of business ownership never happens. Years later he looks back on his life with regret, sorry he never took the risk.

For millions of people like Richard, the basic risk in giving up something familiar keeps them trapped in limited and unsatisfying lives, never achieving their dreams.

Winners take risks

Every day, people do take bold risks and achieve their dreams. A Florida man named John Mautner is such a person. He worked in a comfortable but boring accounting job for 10 years. It seemed risky for him to leave his secure job and pursue his dream of owning a business. His wife, his friends, and even his co-workers told him he would be crazy to take such a chance. But with careful planning he felt confident enough to face risk head on. Eventually, he quit his accounting job and began his dream career of creating and selling specialty snack food. Mautner was ready for risk, because he had planned for it. Before taking that risk, he had spent much of his free time in his kitchen, developing and testing tasty new snack recipes, and his planning, patience, and work paid off. Just three years after making the move to pursue his dream, John Mautner became a millionaire. His snack company, The Nutty Bavarian, now has retail stores across the country. Obviously, nobody calls him crazy now.

When you are confronted by risk, you can face it with the same confidence Mautner displayed. With proper planning you will be ready for most of the challenges risk can bring. Sometimes, moments of risk can appear without warning. At other times, you will have the luxury of being able to choose exactly when you will take a risk. Whatever the timing, expect these risk situations to occur. Sooner or later, as you pursue your goals, you will be forced to take a leap of faith to reach success.

Debbi came from a big family. She longed for praise from her parents, but usually didn't get much. As a result, she grew up with little confidence. Marrying a successful executive didn't change her attitude. While she felt awkward and out of place with his friends, she did feel confident in the kitchen, baking. She longed for success, but getting out there and having the guts and determination to risk failure and humiliation were hard for her to imagine. As time passed, Debbi realized she had to stop dreaming and take the risk to be fulfilled. Not too long ago, she shared with me her family's reaction to this decision:

> *I decided to go into the cookie business. I said to Mom and Dad and my husband, "I'm going to go into the cookie business, because you've always told me how great my cookies are."*
>
> *"Oh, Debbi," they said, "that's such a stupid idea. You'll absolutely fail. It will never work. Give it up." You know, they were telling me things that, frankly, I already believed. But, more important, I never wanted to look back and say, "If only."*

She had her mind set on opening a cookie shop. Her husband predicted failure, but gave her the money for the start-up. The day the store opened, there were absolutely no customers. Debbi was devastated! She had taken a risk and put herself on the line, and it looked like she was headed for failure. She decided her husband had been right. Taking such a big risk had been a mistake! But risk-taking can get easier after you've taken your first big risk, so Debbi decided to take one more.

Normally a shy person, she began walking up and down the street with a tray of hot cookies, offering a taste to passers-by. Of one thing she was confident: Her cookies tasted great. Sales took off, and today Debbi Fields' name is displayed on hundreds of cookie stores. The company is called Mrs. Fields' Original Cookies, and it is one of the most successful bakery chains in the business. Today Debbi Fields glows with an attitude of confidence! So if you lack the confidence to take risks, don't worry. Follow the two keys to risk-taking and you can face this challenge head on.

The first key: prepare for risk

There are two keys to create the confidence you need to face risk. Preparation is the first and most important step to help get you smoothly and successfully past the point of no return, and on your way to your goals. Do not rely on luck to get you through that moment of truth. Luck only happens when preparation meets timing. Spend time each day preparing yourself for the risks you'll face. Take the following steps:

- ◆ Gather and study information about your particular goals.

- ◆ Learn to recognize opportunities and resources that will help you take your leap of faith.

- ◆ Talk to or read about people who've already achieved the goals you have planned. Find out how they overcame the challenges they faced along the way.

- ◆ Prepare now so you will be ready to make your move when the time comes.

Yes, this is a simple concept. Preparation seems like common sense. Nevertheless, many people gloss over it or avoid it, assuming they will somehow be ready when the time comes. Do not assume. Be certain by preparing now.

John Mautner, who became a millionaire by selling snack food, spent an entire year preparing for the moment to take his leap of faith. His free time was spent researching the snack food market and developing his new product. He prepared as much as he could for the changes that he knew would soon happen. Debbi Fields spent a lifetime developing cookie recipes she knew were irresistible. This kind of preparation naturally gives you self assurance. Get as prepared for risk as you can be and you will build a solid foundation of confidence.

The second key: rehearse for risk

The second key to risk planning is *rehearsal*, which is quite different from preparation. While preparation is the process of gathering and studying information and ideas, rehearsal is the *visualization* of successful risk-taking. Preparation and rehearsal work together to give you both the knowledge and the self-confidence you need to overcome the challenge of risk.

Rehearse your future leap of faith by repeatedly visualizing yourself taking that leap and succeeding. See yourself facing risk confidently and winning again and again. Picture yourself standing at that point of no return, then see yourself moving forward boldly toward your goals. As if it is recorded on videotape, watch yourself achieve success, then rewind the entire sequence and watch it again, and again. If fears intrude and images of failure slip into your mind, gently push them away and start again. Visualize the entire sequence of events in your plan from confident start to successful finish. Mentally rehearse your risk-taking and see yourself overcoming risk. But again, don't stop the visualization there. Keep picturing your forward progress all the way to the successful conclusion of your plans.

When facing risk, most people first imagine all the things that could go wrong. Their doubts soon increase as they start asking themselves *what if* questions. What if I fail? What if things don't go just right? What if I end up regretting doing this? What if my life ends up worse than it is now? What if my friends say "I told you so"? Successful people will tell you that it is wise to be prepared for the possibility of failure by having an alternate plan of some kind, but do not waste time rehearsing failure. Visualizing failure only causes your doubts to soar, making any risk seem insurmountable.

Pretend you can do something, and believe it with all your heart, and sure enough, you will find you can do it. The way to create that belief in yourself is to visualize yourself doing it repeatedly. Everyone who reaches for a major goal has to face risks and challenges. The ones who cross these hurdles with the greatest ease not only do their homework, but also mentally rehearse with a passion.

The greatest risk

One of the most common fears is that of public speaking. Surveys reveal that for many people this fear is stronger than the fear of dying. This was definitely true for me. Like millions of others I was terrified at the prospect of having to speak in public. It didn't just give me butterflies; it made me physically ill. To pursue my goals I knew that public speaking was essential, but my complete lack of confidence made me avoid this risk whenever I could. When I was forced by circumstances to speak, my performance reflected my fear. I visualized failure and that was my result, even with the friendliest of audiences. Not that anyone threw tomatoes, but the response was underwhelming and I could feel the audience's uneasiness when I spoke.

Then one day, a talented speaker suggested a way to be better. I didn't realize it at the time, but it involved the two keys—preparation and rehearsal. He told me that the first way to gain confidence was, as he put it, to over-prepare my speech. This meant writing it many weeks in advance if possible, making sure it was perfectly polished, just the right length, and so on. Overprepping also meant practicing the speech in front of a mirror until I knew it inside and out. The second step was to picture myself speaking before a very receptive audience. He suggested I imagine the audience listening raptly and applauding enthusiastically at the end.

So the next time I had to speak, I prepared carefully. Then, I rehearsed the situation mentally, using visualization. I imagined being confident as I spoke. I visualized my speech ending on a high note and the audience applauding loudly. When the day came for my speech, my complete preparation naturally made me more confident than usual, but as I heard my introduction being given, I felt panicky. When I summoned up the rehearsed images in my mind, my confidence returned. As I relaxed, I got into my talk and gave the best performance possible. At the end, the audience even applauded just as I had visualized! Since that time, I've discovered that many professional speakers use similar visualization techniques to give themselves more confidence.

Dottie Walters is an international authority on speaking, and she's co-author, with Lilly Walters, of *Speak and Grow Rich* (Prentice Hall, 1988). During a radio interview she told me of her experience with mental imagery. It was her first speech before an audience of thousands and she was scared stiff. As she waited to be introduced, she began picturing a most comforting object, her child's soft pink comforter. She imagined that pink blanket filling the entire theater, soothing everyone in the audience. Her talk turned out to be a smash hit with several standing ovations from the crowd. Incredibly, a woman came up to Walters afterwards and asked how she managed to get such pretty, pink light to fill the theater during her talk! There was no pink light. Such is the mysterious power of visualization.

Prepare and rehearse to give yourself a confident attitude, and meet the challenge of risk. Get creative and have some fun with your visualization of success. Don't let your fear of risk-taking limit your achievement. Here's an exercise for today: Write down two risks, or leaps of faith, you want to feel more confident about in your quest for your goals. For each of those risks, write down how you can prepare for the challenge it represents. What preparation can you do in the days, weeks, and months ahead that will build your confidence?

Then write down several visual images of success that you can rehearse to give yourself even greater confidence. These should be brief action scenes that picture your successful follow-through and completion of the two risky situations you imagine having to face.

2 risks I anticipate facing

1. _____

2. _____

Ways I can prepare for each of these risks

1. _____

2. _____

Scenes I can mentally rehearse

_____

_____

_____

Remember that confidence is an attitude that can be learned. Every day people face risks and achieve their dreams. You, too, will face risk on your path to success, so learn to have the confident attitude you need to face risk by following through on today's exercise. Prepare fully, then rehearse success mentally with a passion. Prepare and rehearse, and you will be ready when the obstacle of risk appears.

Today's journal

What mattered to me today:

_____

_____

_____

_____

_____

Coincidences, hunches, breakthroughs I experienced today:

_____

_____

_____

_____

New ideas I had today:

_____

_____

_____

_____

My thoughts, feelings, reflections on today:

_____

_____

_____

_____

Turn failure into success

*Go after your dreams with such passion, such spirit, such
determination, and such intensity that you'll
either succeed or explode!*

—Wayne Allyn Root

Today the focus is on conquering lack of persistence, frequently an obstacle to goal achievers. If you've ever given up, quit, or walked away from an important goal, you are not alone. People often make plans to succeed but don't follow through. The good news is that persistence, like any attitude, can be learned. It's an attitude anyone can develop. Because you have stayed with the Countdown all the way to Day 12, it is clear that you have a degree of persistence. You can strengthen and magnify that basic quality into something more powerful that will help you overcome *any* defeat on your path to success.

Very persistent people

Virtually every great achiever in history has shown persistence. On a Sunday in April, young Tiger Woods finished the last hole at

Augusta National to win the 1997 Masters Tournament by the widest margin in history. Though many think he came out of nowhere to wear the legendary green jacket of the champion, his is actually a story of persistence. Woods had spent almost his entire lifetime playing and practicing golf for the chance to play in that very tournament. He'd struggled through the Masters the previous two years, not even breaking par. Had he given up or lost hope as many others do, he would never have become the best in golf, gotten his name in the history books, or collected well over $50 million in endorsements.

Fashion magnate Tommy Hilfiger started out in a modest way: His first clothing store was the trunk of his car. He sold blue jeans to passers-by. Persistence kept him going. He struggled along for years, at one point filing for bankruptcy. But Hilfiger's refusal to give up on his dream is what finally led to his success. Today, his company's annual revenues are $500 million.

There are many more examples of persistence in the history books: Henry Ford, whose original automobile manufacturing business failed after one year; Walt Disney, whose first studio went bankrupt; Michael Jordan, who was cut from his high school basketball team. The list goes on and on. Such stories of persistence abound because everyone who succeeds has to overcome failure.

Hang in there, because:*

♦ The greatest quarterbacks complete only six out of 10 passes.

♦ The best basketball players make only 50 percent of their shots.

♦ Major league baseball players make it to first base only 25 percent of the time—and that includes walks.

♦ Top oil companies, even with the help of expert geologists, dig an average of 10 wells before finding oil.

♦ Successful actors are turned down 29 out of 30 times while auditioning for roles in television commercials.

♦ Winners in the stock market make money in only two out of five investments.

*Source: ABC Fast Fax

Persistence: the success state of mind

Persistence is not something you are born with. It's a state of mind that you create in yourself. It's a way of thinking that keeps you moving forward toward a goal, regardless of defeat or criticism from others. Without persistence, you will never achieve your ultimate goals of success in life.

Some people are defeated by just one major failure in life. That's all it takes to convince them that they were never meant to succeed. Others throw in the towel after just two or three setbacks. For these people, a few painful letdowns are enough to make them give up and stop trying.

Finding joy in failure

There are few contemporary stories of turning failure into success as inspiring as the one told by Wayne Allyn Root in his book *The Joy of Failure!* (Summit Publishing, 1996). He literally failed his way to the top, and proudly proclaims himself to be "The World's Most Successful Failure." Root started failing early, as the youngest losing candidate ever in local politics in his home base of Westchester County, New York. Next, he failed in real estate four times, tried a dozen different careers—all failures, tried to go public with a company and lost his funding, and finally went bankrupt. His personal losses include a divorce (his first wife left him for another man) and the loss of both his parents to cancer within just 28 days of each other. Later on, Root reached for his dream of being a national television broadcaster. Now he estimates this quest caused him to be rejected several thousand times. With a chuckle, Root shared with me what the TV executives, news directors, and producers told him:

> *Everybody said such supportive things as, "Wayne Root is a jerk," "Wayne Root is a joke," "Wayne Root is incompetent," "Wayne Root is amateurish." In the end, what's important is that I won out. I had the last laugh. I proved that one "yes" changes your life. It wipes the whole slate clean, it erases all the "nos."*

Astonishing his detractors, Root was suddenly hired as a television anchorman at a major national cable network. After that success, he went on to found his own business and became a self-made millionaire. Today he lives in Malibu with his wife and family. He earns up to $15,000 a day as a motivational speaker. He has also created a strong spiritual foundation on which to build his life, and is devoted to sharing his personal principles for success with others.

The ones who persist are the ones who get results. Failure almost always precedes success. Ask achievers about failure, and you will hear some amazing stories. Many successful people I have interviewed believe that their defeats gave them the knowledge and perspective they needed to reach their goals.

Champions never give up

In sports, persistence can be directly measured by the number of wins and losses of a team or an athlete. Former Chicago Bears coach Mike Ditka's persistence inspired the Bears to 112 victories and a Super Bowl championship. Ditka's philosophy is "You never really lose until you quit trying."

Reprinted with special permission of North America Syndicate.

Ohio State football coach Woody Hayes achieved 205 Big Ten victories, more than any college football coach in history. His persistence carried the Buckeyes to 11 bowl games, and produced 56 All-American players. Woody Hayes described his philosophy of success in four words: "Paralyze resistance with persistence."

Rick Mears, four-time Indianapolis 500 winner, knows what fuels his success. In the grueling world of long-distance auto racing, persistence is his main ingredient for success. Mears describes the key to victory: "To finish first, you must first finish."

If persistence isn't something you seem to have naturally, do not be concerned. Just like any winning attitude, persistence is a state of mind, and you can develop it if you are willing to make the effort.

Four keys to persistence

So just how can you go about becoming a more persistent person? While studying those who have overcome repeated setbacks and achieved their goals, I have seen the same four keys to persistence over and over again.

First key: belief

The first key to persistence is to truly believe that it is possible to achieve a desired result. Believe in yourself, and believe that you can get what you want. If you are full of doubt, suspend your doubts. In other words, if you find it hard to believe that you can do it, pretend you can do it. Act as if you're certain of success. Acting and pretending will soon lead to actual belief.

Have you ever gotten deeply involved in a movie or TV show because the actors were so believable and the story seemed so real? Without much effort on your part, your emotions and thoughts became focused on the outcome of the story as if it were actually happening. If you have ever experienced this kind of involvement in a work of fiction, then you are perfectly capable of suspending doubt and creating belief about a real-life situation. If you act as if any goal is achievable, you will soon start believing it is achievable.

Build belief in yourself. Here's one technique you can use to create this attitude. It seems so basic that you may wonder if it actually works. Believe me, it does! It helped give me the persistence necessary to achieve many goals, including the writing of this book. (If you have ever written a book, you understand persistence. This book went through many lengthy revisions before it was completed.) Remember that persistence is a state of mind. Believe that you are persistent, and sure enough, you will be persistent. To create this belief in yourself, you must get yourself to believe that you can stay with something challenging without giving up. In other words, if you are persistent about one single thing, you can transfer that same state of mind to the achievement of much greater goals. As those larger achievements are realized, your belief in your persistence will become even stronger. It becomes an upward spiral of positive persistence.

Novice mountain climbers do not start out by climbing Mount Everest. (If they do, the results are often fatal.) Successful climbers first learn to conquer a small mountain, then a larger mountain, and so on. Each triumph builds their confidence, endurance, and strength, until they are ready to face an ultimate challenge such as Everest. It's the same when building persistence. You start small, and build your belief in yourself over time.

Choose a task. Here's how to begin. Think of *one routine task* that you tend to avoid doing every day. You might choose a routine household chore. For example, do you avoid making the bed right away when you get up each morning, or washing the dishes right after you eat, or taking out the trash as soon as it's full? If none of these examples applies to you, then think of another daily activity you tend to put off completing each day. Examples might include reading the newspaper from front to back in one sitting, or filling the dog's dish with water, or cleaning the cat's litterbox, or dusting the furniture. It doesn't matter what the task is, just as long as it's something routine that you now tend to avoid doing. Starting today, make that one daily task an absolute will-do every single day for the next three weeks. Add this task to your daily routine every single day. By the way, do not avoid doing something else because you have added this daily task. It's got to be in addition to your regular daily routine.

How will this make you more persistent? Your completion of the daily task you choose, every day without fail, will not only instill belief, but also self-discipline and self-reliance, and the habit of consistently taking action.

Belief in yourself comes from seeing the visible proof of your persistence every day. It's visible in the bed that is made every day, or in the clean dishes, or in whatever the completed task may be. Anyone can grow this belief by first planting the seed in his or her mind. All it takes is one simple first step, followed by another and another, day after day. There's nothing obsessive or compulsive about being this way. It's a natural, powerful state of mind that is essential for success, and the great thing is, anyone can develop it. Stay with your chosen daily task for the next three weeks. You will soon find yourself applying this state of mind to other areas of your life.

Second key: perspective

The second key is to *gain perspective and knowledge*. Step back from the situation of apparent failure or defeat, and get things in perspective. This may require time or physical distance. Let yourself examine your goal objectively and with as little emotion as possible clouding your vision. If other people fill your head with messages of defeat, remove yourself from those people. Gather all the knowledge you can. Is there anything to be learned from the exact causes of your setback? The key to achieving a goal will sometimes be staring you in the face, but you will never recognize it without perspective.

There have been few failures more graphic than the 1986 Challenger space shuttle disaster. It exploded 73 seconds after takeoff, killing all seven crew members. Within moments of the disaster, NASA investigators began trying to determine exactly what went wrong. The scientists set to work to find out what part of the craft had failed, or what human error had occurred. Their initial investigation took months to complete and involved mind-boggling detail and study. But the facts the investigators uncovered were put to use to reduce the risk for future missions. So even in the aftermath of a failure as big as the Challenger disaster, the perspective and knowledge gained were vital to future success.

You have probably learned some lessons the hard way. As you pursue the results you want, you will learn some important lessons the hard way, through temporary defeat. Once you have gained all the knowledge and perspective you can from those major setbacks, you will be ready for the next key.

Third key: renewal

That third key to persistence is to *renew your energy and focus*. Gather your mental resolve and rebuild your energy for a peak effort ahead. You get focus and resolve through meditation, visualization, prayer, and reflection. You get physical energy from regular exercise, healthy food, and enough rest. All of these things provide you the renewal necessary to achieve victory. If you skip the step of renewal, your next attempt to break through the barrier to your goal may fall short, making you even less certain of success. Recharge your batteries and sharpen your thoughts, so you can give it your highest possible level of performance. And of course, while visualizing and meditating on the challenge, you may suddenly find the answer to help you reach your goal.

Fourth key: action

After renewing your energy and sharpening your focus, move to the fourth key to persistence: *Get into action and go for what you want with total passion!* Reach for what you want to achieve one more time. Make a concentrated effort to go for it one more time, and go for it with all the emotional fire within you. Use persistence to overcome those seemingly insurmountable obstacles that you will face on the way to ultimate success.

How can persistence improve your life?

Persistent people earn the rewards that you, too, can experience. For example, those who are physically fit tend to be persistent about exercising. Those who maintain the widest circle of friends tend to be persistent about staying in touch with all of them. Those who are in jobs they love are often the most persistent about finding the best job they can. Start building a more persistent state of mind, and you will be able to get the results you want in life.

Now it's time for you to discover some ways that being more persistent can improve your life, starting today. Think about some specific areas of your life that will be better if you are more persistent. Here are some examples.

- ◆ Perhaps you could be more persistent about exercise. Applied persistence here would make you look and feel better.
- ◆ Perhaps you could be more persistent about solving a problem at home or at work. The problem lingers because you haven't stayed with it until it becomes resolved.
- ◆ Perhaps you could be more persistent about completing a project or task you have left unfinished.
- ◆ Would greater persistence give you a stronger relationship with a friend, business associate, or family member?

Write down several specific areas of your life that would improve if you applied greater persistence.

5 areas of my life that persistence will improve

1. _____
2. _____
3. _____
4. _____
5. _____

Now that you've identified some areas of your life that will improve with applied persistence, start building a persistent state of mind to get the results you really want.

Choose a daily task and follow through on it every single day for the next three weeks, and give yourself the chance to strengthen your ability to be persistent. When a major barrier stands in your way and you feel yourself starting to give up, use the four keys of belief, perspective, renewal, and action to blast through the barrier and get results.

Today's journal

What mattered to me today:

_____

_____

_____

_____

_____

Coincidences, hunches, breakthroughs I experienced today:

_____

_____

_____

_____

New ideas I had today:

_____

_____

_____

_____

My thoughts, feelings, reflections on today:

_____

_____

_____

_____

Do it now

The world can only be grasped by action,
not by contemplation.

—Jacob Bronowski

Over the last three days you have considered some of the specific obstacles to reaching the success you want. Today you will complete this portion of the Countdown by learning ways to get past the common hurdle of inaction.

Once you get past this roadblock, you can consistently get into action and get things done every day. Yogi Berra in his inimitable way said, "If you don't know where you're going, you'll end up someplace else." Having an understanding of where you're going is just the beginning. To achieve your destiny and live the life you have dreamed of, you have to get moving! Take action and you can achieve your ultimate goals. Sit on the sidelines watching, and nothing significant will happen in your life.

The problem is procrastination

Why don't people do what could make their lives better? Maybe it's fear of criticism, fear of failure, fear of success, or simply fear of the unknown. It seems easier to do nothing than to confront the fear. Sometimes people procrastinate because they are disorganized. Others lack the motivation and dynamic energy to get into action.

Then there are those people who *are* aware of their procrastination, but still avoid taking action and, as a result, suffer needless anxiety. For these people, every day, every week, and every year that goes by on the calendar is a burning reminder that they have not taken the necessary action to achieve their goals. They suffer pangs of guilt. They tell their friends and family all about their dreams and schemes, but nothing ever seems to get off the ground. If, eventually, their guilt and anxiety build to the point where they finally *do* begin to take action, their energy and drive for success have been dissipated by endless delays, and the final results are less than satisfactory. They've missed the window of opportunity!

Procrastination limits your progress. To take control of your life and get what you want, you must consistently take action. Lots of people have excuses for their lack of progress. The winners in life don't have time for excuses, because they are too busy taking action and getting things done.

"Paralysis by analysis"

I had the honor of meeting world champion tennis player Arthur Ashe shortly before his death. He was appearing at a gathering to support a cause that was important to him. Arthur Ashe was battling the deadly disease AIDS, and certainly had every excuse to sit at home and do nothing. But being the champion that he was, Ashe was in action. He was busy getting things done, meeting people, and enlisting them for the causes he supported. Ashe knew that great things happen when people get moving and do something, in life as well as in sports. Later I learned that Ashe had made a study of this concept. He believed that athletes stop achieving when they begin letting excuses replace performance. Ashe even coined a term to describe this syndrome in athletes: *paralysis by analysis.*

Paralysis by analysis is a great way to describe what keeps many people from achieving desired results. Overanalyzing a goal can make it seem more complex and harder to reach than it really is. Intelligent and creative people may struggle with success because they over-think their goals. They think up many brilliant reasons why their goals are unreachable. The result is that they discourage themselves from taking even the first step. Meanwhile, average people with just average smarts skip all the analysis and, instead, take action and get results. The bottom line: Do not paralyze yourself with too much analysis. Stop worrying and start making things happen! As Walter Anderson, author of *The Confidence Course* (HarperCollins, 1997), often reminds his students, "Nothing quells anxiety like action!"

Overcome procrastination

Described below are five ways top achievers overcome procrastination to get things done.

First: set short-term goals

Start your engine by *choosing a short-term goal*. Set a 10-minute goal for yourself, and do something in the next 10 minutes to get you closer to your goal. Simply *do it*, and the immediate results of your action will create momentum. If a 10-minute goal is too high a hurdle to get you moving, then set a five-minute goal and follow the same procedure. Or set a one-minute goal. Or set only a one-movement goal! For example, pick up the pen. Next, pull out some paper. Then, start writing. Any level of decisiveness creates momentum, and once you're making decisions and taking action, momentum will keep you moving forward.

When you feel like procrastinating, start working on something—anything. That's all it takes to give you the momentum to keep going. Once you're in action, it's possible to get a lot accomplished. There is a law in the world of physics known as Newton's First Law of Motion, which states that objects in motion tend to remain in motion. This rule can also be applied to people. When people take action, they find it easier to *stay* in action.

Second: the limited-time state of mind

The second way to get yourself into action is to *get a limited-time state of mind*. Marketers impose deadlines on their promotions to spur consumers into immediate action. You can do the same thing with yourself by creating an *artificial, ultimate deadline* for yourself. Think about what you want to accomplish, and then imagine you have just one year to live. Imagine this deadline is real and use it to get yourself moving. If that doesn't work, then imagine you have just six months to live, or just one month. None of us knows for certain when our life may end. This uncertainty leads us to assume that we have unlimited time. But life is fleeting. Put yourself in a limited-time state of mind, and seize the day, seize the moment. Do it now!

How many times have you heard these familiar commercial refrains: "Order before midnight tonight." "This is a limited-time offer." And the always-popular, "Hurry, sale ends tomorrow!" Limited availability naturally increases demand. Experts in motivation realize how effective deadlines can be in making people take action. You can motivate yourself by imagining an immediate deadline and then pushing yourself to meet that deadline.

Third: the fixed action period

The third way to get yourself into action is to assign yourself a *fixed action period*. Each day or each week, set aside time to devote to nothing but achieving the results you want in life. Choose a fixed length of time, perhaps an hour, and let nothing and no one stand in the way of getting things done during this period. You will find that this fixed action period can keep you on track to your goals.

Many successful people set aside a block of time each day to concentrate on a specific goal. One executive I know was having problems finding the time to monitor his investments consistently. He decided to set aside 30 minutes a day, from 3:00 to 3:30 each afternoon, for nothing but that purpose. Within just a few months his portfolio had significantly increased in value. He says that his investment of 30 minutes a day turned out to be the best investment he has ever made. Whatever your goal, setting aside a fixed action period can help you achieve it.

Fourth: get help to get moving

The fourth way to get into action is to *ask someone you trust for help* to move forward on your goals. Get help clearing a hurdle, and once you have momentum, keep moving forward. Or enlist someone to help you on an ongoing basis. For example, you could ask a close friend to request a weekly progress report from you on your plans, or you could ask a loved one to give you gentle reminders when you start slacking off. But avoid extensive discussions with uninvolved people about your goals. Talking too much about goals instead of actively pursuing them weakens your resolve and slows your progress.

Every productive thought you have contains energy that you can use to reach your goals. Successful people capture this energy on the spot and put it to work for them. When an idea or decision comes along, they take some positive action on the spot, and harness the total energy of that idea or decision. Seize the moment when you have a productive thought. Use the energy you feel to do something to advance yourself toward your goals that very moment. Put it off, and the energy is gone forever.

Fifth: use outside motivation

If the above four steps don't get you into action, access the power of motivational words! Words contain energy, because they are the means by which we turn every mental idea into physical expression. In Genesis, the Bible says, "In the beginning was the Word." This is not simply a metaphor. God's word is actually the creative power behind everything we see. The Bible also says, quoting Jesus, "Don't you know you are gods?" (John 10:34). Whether you want to refer to the universal power source as God, as your higher self, or even as the ultimate force, the fact is that each of us has been blessed with the power to create our future through the words we speak.

Words really matter

When you speak, choose your words carefully, because what you say contains energy. Avoid expressing doubt and fear. Speak with confidence and enthusiasm about what you want to happen in your life. If you put enough conviction into what you say, it will eventually happen for you.

You can improve your ability to make things happen by allowing only positive action words into your consciousness. Stay away from doom-and-gloom people, because they tend to talk about failure. If you catch yourself saying something negative, banish the thought and replace it with a positive one. Read positive books, and listen to uplifting audiobooks and music.

Motivating words do not even have to be audible to be effective. Author Elaine St. James discovered that subliminal audiotapes could help her beat procrastination. I tried them and found that they definitely improved my ability to operate at a peak level. These tapes usually contain audible nature sounds or music, which mask hundreds or thousands of repeated positive affirmations. Your brain receives these positive words and eventually they saturate your subconscious, overwhelming negative tendencies. After a while, you suddenly realize your performance has improved significantly. These tapes can help you in all areas of your life, but two good ones to try are *Stop*

Procrastination and *Peak Performance*, both are available from Alpha-sonics International (800-937-2574). One caveat, these tapes are fairly expensive.

What's stopping you?

You have learned some ways to break through procrastination, but you must be the motivating force for your success. If you are not willing to go for your goals, no one can or will do it for you. You alone have to grab your dreams with both hands if you want to turn them into reality. You are the one who must take command of your power to get things done. It's important to find every possible means of unlocking that power, and that includes knowing what I call your *action motivators* and your *action limiters*, two keys to creating consistent, forward momentum. Understanding these two factors is as important to success as knowing the difference between the accelerator and brake pedals on a car.

Action motivators

Everyone has their personal *action motivators*, certain things that give them a positive, goal-oriented, action state of mind. Think back to times in your life when you scored a big victory, when you achieved something significant, when you felt fired up and hungry to reach a goal. By recognizing the conditions and situations that helped you achieve goals in the past, you can duplicate these conditions and create the same state of mind to power yourself into action.

What motivates you to take action? Take a few minutes now to write down a list of five of your personal action motivators. Consider some examples. Has an inspiring leader in your past helped you achieve a major goal? If so, write this down as one of your action motivators. Did you once achieve a victory because you were part of a great team? If so, write this down. In the past, has an inspiring motivational book or tape fired you up to take action? If so, jot this down on the page. If a good run or exercise makes you feel inspired to tackle goals, put that on your list. Perhaps thinking about your financial future, your children's future, or your family's future spurs you into action. Does thinking about time slipping away motivate you to seize today? What about imagining the freedom success will bring you—does that make you want to get into action? Now, write down at least five motivating forces you have employed in the past to create action and reach goals.

5 of my action motivators

1. _____
2. _____
3. _____
4. _____
5. _____

Next, consider how you could recreate these motivating forces in your life today. For example, if in the past an inspiring leader gave you the power to reach a goal, you might find a mentor or adviser to provide the same impetus. If teamwork kept you in action, think about teaming up with others to get things done. If the passing of time motivates you, set up your work place so that time literally stares you in the face. Get a giant wall calendar and cross off the passing days. If motivational tapes inspire you, keep plenty on hand so you have a constant supply. If exercise motivates you, put exercise on your schedule each day before your goals. If a certain thought, such as your family's future, inspires you to action, write that thought out on a card and post it so you'll see it each day. Now, write down five ways to turn on the power of your action motivators today.

5 ways I can create motivation today

1. _____
2. _____
3. _____
4. _____
5. _____

Once you have identified the specific forces that spur you to take action, put them to work for you. Take steps to activate these motivating forces in your life, and recreate the ideal conditions that brought you past success. Use your action motivators to give yourself forward momentum toward your goals.

Action limiters

All of us have our personal action limiters as well, those situations or conditions that stop us from taking action and getting things done. Consider five of the things that have kept you from reaching important goals in the past. Think about the conditions that seem to have held you back from achievement. Examples of action limiters might include negative stories about business or the economy. Maybe seeing or hearing such news in the past has filled you with doubt and affected your motivation to "go for it." Unfortunately, TV and other media are filled with such stories. Perhaps fear of criticism or doubt in yourself has stopped you from taking action. This is a common limiter many face. Maybe a busy work schedule or family commitments have limited your ability to take action on your goals. What other situations have limited your motivation to succeed in the past? Write five of them down now.

5 of my action limiters

1. _____
2. _____
3. _____
4. _____
5. _____

Now that you see these action limiters in writing, you can avoid their negative effects with planning and determination. For example, if negative news stories affect your motivation, skip those stories in the newspaper, or change the channel when such a story comes on

TV. Although this advice may sound simplistic, many people who are negatively affected by these stories do nothing to avoid them. If feelings of doubt are killing your motivation, you might find some truly inspiring examples of people who overcame doubt, and use these examples to keep you moving. If fear of criticism is keeping you stuck in place, consider the worst possible criticism you can imagine getting, and honestly ask yourself if it would be worth risking that criticism to make your lifetime dreams become reality. Get perspective on your fear of criticism in order to control it. If your daily routine, your social life, or your work hours keep you from getting into action, plan a special time each day that's just for you, even if it's 15 minutes first thing each morning. Use this time to take action to make your dreams come true. Neutralize those action limiters. Do not let them stop you from achieving the success you want and deserve. Take a moment to write down ways to neutralize your five action limiters now.

Ways to neutralize my action limiters

1. _____

2. _____

3. _____

4. _____

5. _____

Get into the game

One of the most popular forms of entertainment today is success-watching. There are magazines, TV shows, and radio shows (such as mine) exclusively devoted to this pastime. Millions of people love hearing about other people achieving their dreams. They take vicarious pleasure in other people's success. They find the stories inspiring, but because they don't follow through on the inspiration, nothing changes in their lives. Sadly, relatively few people in the world ever climb out of the audience of success spectators and actually get to taste success for themselves.

What are the barriers that divide the huge audience of success spectators from the relatively few actual participants in success? Actually, there are no barriers. Anyone is free to get up out of his or her seat and join in the game. In other words, the key factor separating successful people from all others is nothing more than *action*.

Successful people are willing to take action. Other people talk about goals, think about goals, and plan for goals, but don't consistently take action to reach the goals. If you have followed through on today's exercise, you're aware of what motivates you to take action—and on the flip side, what kills your motivation. Use this information to keep yourself in action. If you consistently go for it, nothing will be able to stop you.

Take action!

To wrap up today's chapter, let's make something happen. If you're like most people, you have a fitness goal and it's very likely you have been procrastinating on it. Today is your day to take action on your fitness goal. (Be sure you consult with your doctor before beginning any exercise program.)

If being more physically fit and having a firmer, trimmer body are two of your goals, why not begin an exercise program today? Nearly everybody thinks this is a great idea, but most people do not follow through. Seize the moment now! Do one sit-up, or one jumping-jack, or one toe-touch right this minute. Go ahead, do it right now. *Take this challenge, and do it!*

If you followed through just now with action, that wasn't so hard, was it? If you didn't take action, why not do it as soon as you finish reading today? Then set some specific targets for your fitness improvement and start working toward them. Your increased fitness will lead to more energy, which will help you take action. Whatever your personal definition of success, start working toward it today. Get into action and get the results you desire.

Today's journal

What mattered to me today:

_____

_____

_____

_____

_____

Coincidences, hunches, breakthroughs I experienced today:

_____

_____

_____

_____

_____

New ideas I had today:

_____

_____

_____

_____

My thoughts, feelings, reflections on today:

_____

_____

_____

_____

_____

Expand your horizons

The meticulous spender had a little black book. He kept track of every single penny he ever spent. He only had one problem, he never stopped to add it up, and the same thing is true with a network.

—Harvey Mackay

Our obstacles are behind us and now we return to our exploration of the pathways to success. Today, you'll discover a path that's made of the people you know now and those you will know in the future.

Multiply your thought power

Success rarely happens in isolation. Reaching your ultimate lifetime goals of success will likely require interaction with other people. Today's chapter makes this fact a path in itself. It is a well-traveled route, followed by many who have achieved seemingly impossible results. When you reach out and expand your support and influence, you become a more powerful person. One mind alone has tremendous power, but that power multiplies when combined with the thoughts of others. Connect with others and you get powerful results.

You're already powerful

No doubt you've heard the term *networking,* a buzzword in business. Networking is the process of connecting with others for future, mutual gain. Your network consists of the key people you can turn to for help in reaching your goals. Unfortunately, some people think of networking as little more than shaking hands, collecting business cards, and keeping the cards handy in case they need a new job. Imagine going beyond such basic business networking and tapping a far wider and deeper spectrum of contacts to help you achieve results you haven't even imagined yet. If this idea seems farfetched, consider the fact that most people know, on average, between 200 and 300 people. These contacts represent a powerful resource you have for success!

Perhaps you think you don't have that many contacts or know that many people. Let's do a quick exercise designed to find out just how wide and deep your existing network is. Don't worry, you won't have to write down 300 names! You will just make a check mark to represent each person you can think of. To help comb your memory, consider the number of people you already know from different stages or areas of your life: family, school, neighborhood, career, and friends.

First, think of all the people you know in your family, both immediate as well as extended family. Immediate family includes spouse, children, brothers, sisters, parents, and grandparents. Extended family includes uncles, aunts, cousins, nieces, nephews, in-laws, and so on. As rapidly as you can count the faces in your mind, *put a separate check mark in the space provided below* to represent each and every person in both your immediate and extended family. Refer to your address book if necessary.

The people in my entire family

When you're done with the family category, move on to the school category. Again, as rapidly as you can, scan the faces and names in your mind and put a check mark in the space provided to represent each you once knew, or still know, from your school years. Include all those people you can recall: classmates, teachers, coaches, administrators, and so on, from elementary and high school as well as college and graduate school.

The people I know from school

_____

_____

_____

_____

_____

Next, consider all the people you know in your neighborhood. Include neighborhood acquaintances, clergy, perhaps even your mail carrier or the person at the corner store. For everyone whose name and face you know in your neighborhood, put down a check mark. If you live in an apartment building, you might also list your superintendent, maintenance man, or others you know by name and face. Again, feel free to refer to your address book to refresh your memory.

The people I know in my neighborhood

_____

_____

_____

_____

_____

Now, think about your career. Consider the people you work with and the people you've worked with in the past. Include co-workers, your boss, your boss's boss, staff, and support personnel you know. Include those you deal with through work, such as clients and vendors. You might want to pull out that pile of business cards you've collected over the years and flip through them. Now, for everyone you know by name and face in your career, put down a check mark.

The people I know in my career

_____

_____

_____

_____

_____

Finally, if you haven't yet counted all your friends and acquaintances under any of the previous categories, now is the time to count them. Put check marks below representing each of those friends. This list might include those who live in other cities or people who live across town. They may be ones you keep in touch with by phone or by sending letters or a card during the holidays.

My friends and acquaintances

_____

_____

_____

_____

_____

The last step is to add up all the check marks and find out just how many people you actually know. You will probably be amazed, as most people are, to discover the hundreds of acquaintances you actually have. While you may not be in touch with many of these people, and may not have spoken to them for years (or even *want* to contact some of them!), each of them has a connection to you. These connections are valuable resources for your success.

Unleash the power of your network

Now that you have gone through the process of mentally reviewing your personal network of friends, family, and acquaintances, begin putting this resource for success to work for you. Right now, choose five people you know who might be able to assist you in achieving your goals, and write down their names.

5 people I know who may help me achieve success

1. _____

2. _____

3. _____

4. _____

5. _____

Plan to contact all five of these people during the coming week. That's only one phone call a day, something you can certainly fit into your schedule. Make the commitment to make personal contact with one person each weekday. You will be surprised at how willing many of these people will be to assist you if you approach them in the right way. As you make each call, have a mind-set of openness, sharing, and mutual benefit. Ask yourself, what can this person offer me, and equally important, what can I offer them? Keep notes on each conversation. Something that seems irrelevant today may prove important tomorrow.

Importance of networking

One person who is an expert on networking is Harvey Mackay. His first book, *Swim With the Sharks Without Being Eaten Alive*

(Morrow, 1988), has been published in 80 countries and 35 languages. He credits networking for his success as an author of books that sell by the millions, and for his success as CEO of an envelope manufacturing company. Mackay has written a fine book on the subject, *Dig Your Well Before You're Thirsty* (Doubleday, 1997). It's packed with stories and examples that show the ways networking can make or break you, with practical advice for building one of your own. He defines a true network as being not more than one phone call away from the person to help you in any situation.

Recently, Mackay and I sat down to tape a radio interview about the importance of networking. Here's what he had to say.

A network can, without question, form a kitchen cabinet for you.

You can bounce all kinds of ideas off your kitchen cabinet. I happen to have a kitchen cabinet of eight people. Not only do I get good advice from them, but when they have problems, I learn from them.

I have studied all the successful people I've encountered in my lifetime, and I believe the one common denominator is people who have really, truly been able to build and cherish a network of contacts.

I was unknown nationally. I was from Minnesota, and I went out and networked my way to a lot of endorsements on the first book: Billy Graham, President Gerald Ford, Ted Koppel, Gloria Steinem, Lou Holtz.

There's a chapter in Dig Your Well Before You're Thirsty *called "Six Degrees of Separation," meaning you're only six phone calls away from virtually anyone.*

While writing *Dig Your Well* Mackay decided that one person he wanted to interview was boxing great Muhammed Ali. Using his networking skills, Mackay was soon invited to spend the day at Ali's house! Whatever your goals, the contacts you nurture in your network can help make it happen.

The hidden ways others can help you

Dozens of people you know already have skills, ideas, resources, or knowledge to help you achieve results. One of your school friends may now be a valuable business contact who can put you in touch with the person at the top in a particular corporation. A relative may be able to suggest a source of capital through a banker she knows. The person at the corner store may have some insight on small business ownership, or have word of a new local business opportunity. A former co-worker might want to hire you as a consultant. The possibilities are infinite, but our usual tendency is to dismiss the people we once knew as irrelevant to our future goals. Successful people do not regard anyone as unimportant. They seek opportunities and knowledge actively from everyone possible.

The right attitude

Here's an important point: Do not use your contacts just to further your own cause. Progress comes when you connect with others for mutual, shared benefit. Make each contact with an honest attitude of trust and sharing, not one of guile or manipulation. If you take unfair advantage, communication will end and you will lose a potentially valuable contact.

Set the stage for results

Take the time to reestablish old relationships. Become reacquainted. Listen and learn about the other person's interests, needs, and concerns. Take notes! Tell him or her you want to stay in touch on a more frequent basis in the future. Then follow up! Call again in a month or two, and always make your agenda simple and clear: Share any news of interest, offer your time and services, be a friend. You are cultivating a contact for the future, and this requires an investment of time and sincere interest. This contact sets the stage for all that is to come, so establish a strong sense of mutual, shared benefit. Again, keep notes on your conversations for reference. Once you've established some contacts, or rebuilt some contact that may have faded over time, you have started building the framework for what will one day become a strong network.

Just one key synergistic relationship can completely change your life for the better and catapult you toward your goals. It is hard to believe the power of a strong personal network. To create it only takes the effort to reach out and follow through. From those you least expect, you may receive the greatest benefit.

Enhanced communication

If networking is your path to success, there is one important skill that must be emphasized.

Expanding your horizon is a pointless exercise if you are an ineffective communicator. Many people only realize a fraction of their potential as communicators. Most convey information at a level that gets them through life, but which hinders their ability to achieve their ultimate goals. Improve your ability to communicate adequately, and you'll improve your chances of achieving success through others.

You communicate with the world through *reading, writing, speaking,* and *listening.* You learned reading and writing as a child in school. While these skills are important, most educated people read and write well enough to achieve results. Speaking one-on-one is also something most people do fairly well, because they do it constantly. One-on-one is the most common way you will speak in a network. You can improve both your personal and public speaking skills by building a richer vocabulary and learning how to get your ideas across to a group. But the most dramatic enhancement in communication comes from improving the skill that is often overlooked: listening.

Good listening requires focus. Unlike writing or talking, good listening demands that we adjust fully to the *other person's* style of communication. To absorb all the information being offered, we have to adjust ourselves to the speaker's pace, style, and point of view. We have to filter out the verbal and visual distractions, and focus on the message and the meaning. Because most of us have never been taught how to do this, we listen ineffectively, resulting in poor communication and missed opportunities.

What are you missing?

Below are six warning signs that you need to improve your listening skills. If any of these warning signs sound familiar to you, the good news is that you have a terrific opportunity to improve how you communicate with others.

1. You *interrupt* others before they finish their thought. Interrupting limits the complete expression of thoughts and ideas.

2. The *"I've heard everything"* syndrome. Rushing to judgment or picking apart thoughts leads to missed knowledge and opportunities.

3. The *"Can you top this?"* syndrome. Jumping in with a topper to show you know more than someone else results in one-sided communication.

4. You *hide* instead of listen. Hiding behind your desk, your voice mail, or your secretary at work, or hiding behind the newspaper or TV at home limits your chances to listen and learn.

5. You *listen to yourself.* Thinking about what you just said and coming up with your next brilliant statement can cause you to miss what others are trying to tell you.

6. The *"Shut up and listen"* syndrome. You refuse to listen, which inevitably leads to disaster. One-way conversation isn't communication.

Think about how you listen. There may be room for improvement in your listening skills. People will gladly share their deepest thoughts and feelings with you if you are willing to really listen to them. The value of your network will grow as you become a better listener.

The essence of good listening

Review the six warning signs and you will notice that most of these behaviors stem from focusing on what you are saying, instead of focusing on what the other person is saying. In other words, the essence of good listening simply means talking less and listening more. The ancient Greek philosopher Epictetus wrote, "Nature has given to us one tongue but two ears, that we may hear from others twice as much as we speak." With that thought in mind, take this challenge to become a better communicator during the next two days.

Spend a few hours face-to-face with a friend sometime over the next two days, and take the time to really listen to what that person has to say to you. As you listen, consider the meaning of what is said before you form a response. Don't rush to fill the gaps in the conversation. Begin forging deeper and more meaningful relationships with those close to you by being a more receptive listener.

Release all judgment

There is one more step to receptive listening, and that is to release yourself from all judgment of what others say to you. Let go of your ego's desire to pigeonhole, judge, or relate everything to your own experience. Adopt the point of view of a completely receptive student, even when listening to the youngest child. Be open to and understanding of other people's perceptions of the world.

When parents want to communicate closely with a child, they often adjust their stance to put their eyes on the same level as the child's eyes. Receptive listening means doing the same thing with your *point of view*. Adjust your point of view to the other person's, even if it is a challenge. Look at the world from their perspective. You will learn things you didn't know and you will benefit from each of these encounters.

Now, cross off another day on your calendar as you make a vow to expand the horizons of your world.

Today's journal

What mattered to me today:

_____

_____

_____

_____

_____

Coincidences, hunches, breakthroughs I experienced today:

_____

_____

_____

_____

_____

New ideas I had today:

_____

_____

_____

_____

_____

My thoughts, feelings, reflections on today:

_____

_____

_____

_____

_____

Learn
from leaders

*Look for someone who has that Midas touch, that Houdini
or Stradivari quality that will really inspire you,
motivate you, and guide you.*

—Terri Sjodin

Today's path explores seeking out one or more very special people
to guide you to your dreams. Successful people have much to teach us
about achievement. These people set standards of excellence that can
inspire us to reach higher in every part of life. You can learn the steps
to achieve many ambitious goals simply by learning from and model-
ing yourself after successful people. Learning from leaders is a great
way to speed your progress toward any goal, while at the same time
adding meaning to your quest for success.

A leader to learn from

David and his dad often went out to dinner together, and that led
to the boy's fascination with the restaurant business. By age eight, he
knew what his life's work would be. As a teenager, he worked as a

busboy, then later as a short-order cook. He even married a waitress! Then, a key event occurred that was to change his life forever. He had a chance meeting with leading fast-food entrepreneur Colonel Harlan Sanders. That meeting led Sanders to became a mentor to Dave. Soon the young man was offered a job with Kentucky Fried Chicken, where he learned all he could from the Colonel about success in the quick-service food industry. Dave used that knowledge to build his vision of success. A few years later, he took a leap of faith and opened his own restaurant. As you may have already guessed, Dave's full name is Dave Thomas. His first restaurant, Wendy's, named for his daughter, has grown to a chain of 4,500 stores. Today the company is a $3-billion empire.

The first step: study a successful formula

You can learn from leaders by seeking someone who has achieved the results you want and learning from his or her winning actions. It's not necessary to reinvent the wheel to get to your goals. No matter what you want to achieve, it is a sure bet that someone, somewhere has already achieved those same goals, or at the very least, goals similar to yours. Use their performance as a guideline and you will get what you want.

As you know, the goal of this book is to help you discover your personal path to success. Do not confuse the uniqueness of your path with the means you can use to discover it. For example, while a man could travel to a special one-of-a-kind destination, he can still drive an automobile to get there. An artist could create a totally fresh and unique painting, but he doesn't have to invent a brand new paint brush to do it. As you seek out your unique path and personal goals, you may for a time wisely choose to use a trail already blazed by a mentor. Of course, you are always free to set a different course, find a new path, or select new goals whenever you want.

Time and again people trying hard, only to see their dream run smack into a brick wall, because they had not bothered to learn how others have achieved the same goal. Why don't more people follow this obvious strategy for success? Perhaps many avoid using role models because their egos convince them their own ideas are better. Plus, they've been fooled by all the stories of rugged individualists, the ones who "did it their way." You are very unique, but do not confuse your individuality or your unique path with the goals you want to achieve. No matter what your goals, it is likely they have been reached in some form by others before you. Therefore, you can gain valuable knowledge by studying the successful formula that has worked for others in reaching those goals.

The second step: find a mentor

If the idea of *learning from leaders* resonates with you, take it a step further by finding a mentor who can provide you with personalized, highly valuable guidance and wisdom. Becoming a protégé of a mentor is the most powerful way to learn from leaders, because you receive their hard-earned advice and information each step of your journey.

Imagine that you are in a foreign country without a map, and all the road signs are in a language you don't know. You ask questions, but nobody understands. No one can give you directions. How can you ever reach your destination? You can either stumble along blindly until you find it, or you can get yourself an experienced guide. Obviously, finding someone who knows the country, the short cuts, and the fastest routes would be valuable to you. That is exactly the role a mentor can play in helping you attain success.

How to find a mentor

Terri Sjodin is someone who has built a successful career as an entrepreneur, author, and speaker, thanks to the mentors who guided her. When I recently interviewed her for my show, here's what she said about the process of finding such a special person:

> *Frustration comes from knowing what you want but not having any idea how to get it. So the very first thing you have to do is really hone in on what you want to do and then start to focus on people who are already successful at it. Once you start reading about them, the things that they've done, the paths*

they've taken, you say to yourself, "What things would I really enjoy doing that they've done to help me get where I want to go?" Then, as you start to move along that path, start to let everybody know that's what you want to do.

As soon as you start putting out the word, mentors will be drawn to you. Then you try to set up interviews with the people who have already accomplished your goals. Meet, research, interview, and then follow through to begin a mentoring relationship with someone who has that Midas touch.

Sjodin told me that what she calls the "Law of Attraction" works naturally when you begin to model your behavior after that of successful people. You will soon find these people showing up in your life. A familiar Zen proverb is "When the student is ready, the teacher will appear." The teacher, your prospective mentor, might appear to you as the author of a magazine article, as a speaker at a seminar, or as someone mentioned to you by a friend. Once you make the decision to pattern your actions after those who have achieved desired results, stay alert for one or more mentors showing up in your life.

Terri Sjodin is co-author of *Mentoring* (Irwin, 1997), written with her speaking mentor Floyd Wickman. It's a complete guide to the process of finding or being a mentor or protégé. By the way, don't assume that finding your mentor will be easy. As with any worthy endeavor, there is effort involved. Sjodin talked about it.

Of all my mentors, 99 percent were not interested in mentoring me, or were very busy. My job was to sell them on why it would be worth their time to invest in me.

As the protégé, you obviously get the first return on the investment. But the mentor does get benefits over the long run. For example, Floyd helped me initially with my speaking work. But he had never had a book in the bookstores. Because I had already accomplished that, I could bring something new to the table as our relationship evolved.

Connecting with a mentor is a powerful step forward. It requires effort and commitment, but the payback from a mentoring relationship can be highly rewarding.

Steps to success

To begin the process, identify others who have reached some goals that you have identified and then explore the steps to success that they used. You have already laid the groundwork for this earlier in the Countdown, by listing what results you want to achieve. As you think about a specific goal, plan on doing some research on people who have already reached that same goal. You may very possibly know, or know about, one or more successful people who have done what you dream of doing. If there is a specific book or article written by that person, that's your first step. Get that information and absorb it! If not, then learn all you can about this leader's steps to success through other means. Visit the library, search the Internet, ask experts. Do whatever it takes to gather the data you need.

For example, let's say your dream is to be the financially secure owner of a specialty mail order catalog business. Lillian Vernon is an excellent role model in this field. She has written a book titled *An Eye for Winners* (HarperCollins, 1996) that is filled with information about how she did it. The fact is, today we are in the midst of an information explosion. There are books, magazines, and newsletters on every conceivable subject by nearly anyone you can think of. Just because you have never heard of a publication in your area of interest, do not assume none exists. Check your local library reference desk for books such as *Newsletters in Print* or *Gale Directory of Publications*. In a few minutes' time you can discover new sources of information on the steps to success you can take.

Keep a watchful eye

Once you have researched how others achieved the results you want, start patterning your actions after theirs. During this process, stay alert to opportunities to connect with one or more mentors. Once you are on this path, the universe will automatically bring mentors into your life, but you must be watchful or you may miss the chance to make contact. Of course, you can help things along if you already have a mentor in mind. Get in touch with that person and ask him or her for a few minutes of time. Prepare for your meeting by creating a list of some specific questions to ask. Keep careful notes on the answers you receive and follow through. You might study Sjodin's book for more tips on these important first steps.

You may not know of anyone who has already achieved exactly the same goal that you want to achieve. If, after searching the library and your list of friends and acquaintances, you just cannot come up with a name or names, then you can leave it up to the universe to bring these people into your life. But do not be passive; stay alert, and while you wait, make it your assignment to continue seeking people who have successfully reached the goal you have identified.

Remember, these people you seek had to overcome the same doubts and fears you feel. They had to break through the same barriers that you face. Draw knowledge and inspiration from them. You might motivate yourself by displaying some pictures of your role models. Framed photographs, letters, mementos, or artwork can all be reminders of those who inspire you and can provide you with a constant spark of motivation. It may smack of adulation, but it's not silly if it works.

Have some heroes

Along with the knowledge you can get from mentors, you can gain inner strength by having personal heroes. Everyone needs heroes, especially now, when many in the media examine every human flaw they can find. The simple truth is that everyone is imperfect, even heroes. Do not expect to find flawless perfection in anyone, because you will be disappointed. Make it your mission to discover the heroic qualities in those you admire, and to be inspired by their strengths. Leaders who inspire you can change the course of your life and help you see that your boldest dreams are within reach.

Find someone to inspire you

The rare opportunity to meet someone you consider inspiring is a chance not to be missed. Anyone who has had this experience will tell you that it can energize and motivate. Seek opportunities to actually speak with or meet with some of those special people who, as Mark Twain says, "make you feel that you, too, can become great."

There is a special quality about such positive people. Their energy and charisma is infectious and they can give others the motivation to reach higher. It's not necessary to meet or talk with them to catch their spark. You can access their energy in other ways.

Leaders are always available

Inspiring, knowledgeable leaders are always available. Their thoughts lie waiting on the pages of books—from the guiding thoughts of spiritual leaders, to master works of great philosophers, to new insights from today's visionaries—all are available in libraries and bookstores. There are magazines that profile leaders who have taken paths to success. One of my favorites, appropriately enough, is *Success* magazine. You can also learn from leaders through audio and video tapes, as well as from seminars and speeches. Jot down the inspiring words and beliefs you learn from these people. When your path seems difficult to travel, turn to these words for fresh energy and motivation.

Failures can inspire us

You may look at a leader and assume that person is naturally successful. But everyone, even your role models and heroes, had to face weaknesses, shortcomings, and challenges. Sometimes they overcame obstacles more daunting than you can imagine. Learning about the early failures and disappointments of the people you admire, and knowing how they overcame their most difficult challenges, can give you even greater inspiration.

A man whose childhood was less than perfect was raised by a series of nannies hired by his cold and remote parents. After he was sent away to school, his father scolded him for writing letters that began with "Dear Papa." His father insisted that he be addressed as "Father" in all future letters. Nothing the boy did was good enough for his parents. He was reprimanded constantly and told he was sloppy, lazy, and unproductive. As a young man he had serious financial problems. He borrowed against his allowance and had to pawn his valuables. As a speaker, he was ridiculed and criticized for being unsophisticated. He had a serious speech impediment that took years of training to correct. Sometimes he became very depressed and would turn to alcohol to drown his sorrows.

Later in life, he ran for political office and lost. People considered him an eccentric, but a persistent one! Running for office a second time, he succeeded. Yet in times of political crisis, he was known to withdraw, and in private he would break down and cry, pouring out his anguish and doubt. Despite the struggles he had endured and all his many flaws as a human being, he is one of the great leaders of the 20th century and today is a hero to millions. He is the man who inspired his countrymen through their finest hour. Winston Churchill, Prime Minister of England, led his nation to victory in World War II.

Appropriately enough, Churchill once defined success as "the ability to go from failure to failure with no loss of enthusiasm." The trials that heroes endure to reach success can teach us powerful lessons about our own lifetime quest.

The greatest of leaders

Tapping into the knowledge of mentors can show you how to reach success. Personal heroes can provide you with a good measure of inspiration and motivation. Beyond mere mentors and heroes, however, are the greatest of leaders. These rare and wonderful people can change your state of being by their thoughts, words, and guidance. They can lift you to a higher place by revealing an inner light that goes beyond results and goals. Their words and deeds transcend the mundane everyday world. Such leaders can impart *values and beliefs* for living that lead to unlimited results. Who are these people? The great spiritual leaders, saints, sages, and other highly enlightened people who are alive today or who live on in our hearts. Their mission in life is always to lead others out of the darkness into the light, and they stand waiting to do the same for you.

Without a belief system to guide you and values to live by, the material success you achieve will be hollow and short-lived. You can discover your personal philosophy for living by adapting the most meaningful beliefs of the greatest leaders you admire. By anchoring yourself to a system of core beliefs and values, your success can have lasting meaning and you will weather the inevitable storms of adversity, because you will have principles for living to support and guide you.

Find your own principles for living

Do you have a personal philosophy that guides you each day on the road to success? You have read the quotes at the beginning of each chapter, and no doubt you have read hundreds of inspiring quotes through the years. Now, it's your turn! Creating a personal philosophy in just one or two sentences can be highly meaningful. I invite you to take the time to do this today. Borrow an idea from leaders who teach and inspire you if you wish. Use their great words as your guiding principles and craft your own philosophy from their ideas. Or be completely original! Either way, this can be a challenging and rewarding exercise. Writing your personal philosophy in distilled form can teach you a lot about yourself. It may also serve as both anchor and guidepost for you as you read it again in the months and years ahead. Someday, perhaps your words will serve as an inspiration to others who follow your path.

My own words to live by

_____

_____

_____

_____

_____

_____

_____

Today's journal

What mattered to me today:

_____

_____

_____

_____

_____

Coincidences, hunches, breakthroughs I experienced today:

_____

_____

_____

_____

New ideas I had today:

_____

_____

_____

_____

My thoughts, feelings, reflections on today:

_____

_____

_____

_____

_____

Listen to your heart

We have a part of ourselves that guides us away from danger and toward success and fulfillment. That's our internal guidance system.

—Nancy Rosanoff

You've come to the end of week number two in the Countdown. It's another seventh day in the Countdown, a time to pause and reflect before moving ahead to the final week. Seven days ago you considered the real meaning of success and focused on the things in your life that are worth celebrating right now.

Today is about listening to your heart, and heeding that quiet inner voice that some call *intuition*. There are some very successful people who naturally use their intuition. Alfred Sloan, the former president of General Motors, once said, "The final act of business judgment is intuitive." Albert Einstein, Winston Churchill, Buckminster Fuller, and many other renowned people throughout history reportedly used their intuition to make important decisions and achieve results.

In the Western world, most people are brought up to believe that rational thinking is the only correct way to think. Children are taught the scientific method, principles are stated in absolute terms, and rules are fixed on how the world operates. Inner voices or inner guidance are generally considered fantasy and are discouraged. As a result, most of us have lost touch with our natural-born intuition. But this skill can be recaptured if we are willing to tune in and listen.

The voice within

Inside you is a quiet knowing that can help you, but you must be willing to relax, suspend your doubts, and tune in to your heart. Your inner voice can give you answers to your most difficult questions, expand your awareness, and transform your life. Susan Jeffers, author of *Feel the Fear and Do It Anyway* (Fawcett, 1987), is someone who listened to her heart, and it helped open the door for her to become a best-selling author and popular speaker. She shared the following story with me:

> The idea came into my head, "Go to the New School." I'd never been to the New School for Social Research, in New York, but the message came into my head. I got up, went to my secretary and said, "I'm going to the New School."
>
> "Why?" she asked.
>
> "I don't know," I said, and took a taxi to the New School. When I got there, I looked at the building and said, "OK, what do I do now?" Something inside me led me through a number of steps to an empty reception area, where a woman yelled to me, "Can I help you?"
>
> The words that jumped out of my mouth startled me. "I'm here to teach a class on fear," I said.
>
> She looked at me in shock. "My gosh, I've been searching for somebody to teach a class on fear and today's the last day to put it into the catalog!"
>
> That was really a change in my whole direction in life and started the ball rolling on my writing and teaching.

If you are a skeptic, you might scoff and dismiss this story as strange, weird, or coincidental. Those who have learned to rely on their inner voice to guide them are convinced that intuition is both very real and perfectly natural. I've been using the term inner voice, but don't get hung up on the idea that intuition is an audible voice. The subtle messages of your heart can come to you in many forms. You might actually hear a voice, or have a thought, idea, or phrase pop into your head. You might be impressed by an image or word in your mind. A vivid picture might appear on your mental screen. You may have a feeling, a sense of knowing. A right or wrong decision might be sensed physically, as a "gut instinct" or a feeling in the pit of the stomach. For some lucky people, intuitive information flows easily and often; for others, this inner source of information needs to be nurtured for it to blossom. It takes patience, a quiet mind, and regular practice. It also helps if you are willing to follow the urging of your inner guidance, as this helps keep the intuitive thoughts coming.

Open your mind

A good first step is to *believe that it is possible* to receive inner guidance. You may already believe that intuition exists. Many people have had the experience of making a decision based purely on gut instinct, and have been pleasantly surprised when it turned out to be the correct choice. This is intuition and it can become a major resource for you.

On the other hand, you might be a doubter. You may have trouble believing that answers to difficult questions can be found within you. If so, remember that the reason you are reading this book is to learn some new ideas that can help make you more successful. A significant number of successful people use their intuition actively each day, and are convinced beyond any doubt that it works. I recently heard about a construction executive who used profit and loss figures to choose the jobs he would bid out. This method wasn't working too well, because he often chose the wrong jobs and lost money. Then he tried using intuitive skills to make each final decision. His profits are now soaring, because he rarely makes a wrong choice. Imagine how much the quality of your life would improve if you could make better decisions consistently.

Check your journal

Since Day 21 of the Countdown, you have been keeping a daily journal. Take a few minutes to look back at your entries from the last two weeks, especially under "Coincidences, hunches, breakthroughs I experienced today." If you have been noticing a lot of these events, it may be a sign that you are tuning in to the subtle forces that are here to guide you. For you, intuitive messages may come easily and be received with little effort. Some of the events you have recorded in your journal might be messages providing clues for the direction and path you should follow. Perhaps you have already been led down new paths in response to these experiences.

If you have only experienced a few coincidental or breakthrough events, or none at all, do not be concerned. Getting on your right path toward success will soon lead to these happening for you. However, be certain your own skepticism about such infinite possibilities isn't a barrier. If you doubt seriously that such breakthroughs can occur, you put a wall between yourself and miracle-making. A little skepticism is healthy, but too much can impede you. Suspend your doubts. Give yourself the freedom to believe that anything is possible when it involves your success!

Intuition is information

Nancy Rosanoff, author of *Intuition Workout* (Aslan Publishing, 1988) and an audio program, *Use Your Intuition* (Rosanoff & Associates, 1996), knows many ways to listen to your heart. During a fascinating broadcast interview, she repeatedly stressed to me that one's intuition is a gold mine of information. Here's what Rosanoff said:

> We have analytic minds, which is very good. But we also have a whole realm of nonanalytic data that usually gets left out of the decision-making process. There is a way to incorporate that and increase your chances of making a successful decision.
>
> You do not want to second-guess yourself. On the other hand, if you really do feel uncomfortable with a decision, that feeling

is what I call nonanalytic data. It's telling you something important, that maybe there's something you've overlooked.

I asked Rosanoff whether she thought intuition is easier for women because of "woman's intuition."

Women are intuitive.... But I think they're just more comfortable talking about their intuition than men are. Believe me, men are equally intuitive!

With that stereotype very firmly dismissed, she went on to explain a few easy ways to develop one's natural intuitive ability. Rosanoff teaches seminars to help people access their intuition. Her techniques are quite extensive and varied, but they all lead in one direction. Here she shares just a few ideas for building intuitive perception.

Intuition is like a muscle. The more you exercise it, the better it gets. First, before you do anything, ask yourself, "How do I really feel about this?" And just wait for a feeling response.

If you don't get a physical response, try writing your feelings on a piece of paper without really thinking about what you're writing, and see what comes out.

Or imagine that in one hand you're holding the word yes, and in the other hand you're holding a no. Phrase the question as a yes or a no question and imagine what the words feel like and look like in your hands.

As she explained, these imaginative techniques are designed to connect your inner feelings with your senses of touch, sight, and physical feeling. Rosanoff suggested linking the "yes" and "no" words in your hands to your other senses as well:

Bring them up to your ear and imagine what it would feel like to hear them being said. Finally, take a bite out of each of these words, one at a time, and taste it. Then swallow it and see how it feels going down.

You are giving your whole sense system a chance to respond to the question. You're getting out of your analytic head and you're getting into your intuitive sense.

If you are receptive and open to the sensory messages, the positive or negative sensations you get from these techniques can help you make the right decision. What makes intuition work? Rosanoff thinks there may be something metaphysical at work that allows us to pick up these inner messages.

> *I believe that, somehow, intuition is what connects us as individuals to a greater whole that we are all a part of. That's how we can know the future before it happens. That's how we can be sensitive to someone that we care about. We just have to hear them say hello and we know there's something going on. Or we just have to think about someone and we get a sense of what's going on with them. We have these abilities and we are somehow all connected.*

Intuitive thought is indeed a powerful tool that is used every day by highly successful people. It puts you in touch with a deeper source of knowing that can help you make the right choices. All you have to do it listen to your heart.

You can change your mind

The good news about most life-changing decisions is that they are reversible. You can change careers, you can change your relationships, you can change your goals, and you can even change your life mission. If you've made a bad choice in the past (and who hasn't?), you do not always have to live with that choice. You suffer only when you fail to reverse a bad decision and let opportunities pass. That is when regret and disappointment can haunt you years later, when you run out of time to make things right.

Life's choices

Here's an example of how intuition can help you with life's big choices. Let's say your reasoning mind has led you to decide that a big job offer in another city is right for you. There is a lot more money involved, a jazzy new title, and lots of responsibility. Outwardly, this decision seems like a no-brainer. However, when you test this decision with your intuition, something doesn't feel right about it. You have a gut feeling it's not a good move. You try the yes-and-no test, and it keeps coming up no. Nevertheless, friends and family tell you you're imagining things and so you go ahead with the new job. Six months later you realize you cannot stand the job and the town you have moved to is not what you hoped for, so you move back home. If you had had listened to your intuition, you would have avoided a major mistake.

As far as intuition's role in choosing relationships goes, you only have to look as far as the advice column of your daily newspaper. Nearly every day there's a letter from someone describing a bad relationship. "If only I'd listened to my intuition," the lament goes.

Review those big decisions

You can undo bad decisions, but you do not have to make poor choices in the first place. Right now, think about the major choices you are making regarding success. These will include your life mission, your specific goals, and what you hope to achieve. Your analytic mind may be screaming at you that every choice you have made is absolutely right. Quiet these thoughts for a few minutes. You already know what your rational brain thinks is right.

Further, set aside the real and imagined opinions of other people. Your family and friends have their points of view on success, but you aren't planning to invest all this time and effort just to impress others, are you? This is *your* life we are talking about, and these choices have to be absolutely right for you. If you make wrong decisions, you are the one who will have to pay for it in the end, not the advice-givers.

Listen to your heart and weigh what each of your important life-changing choices really means to you at gut level. Use the intuitive techniques mentioned above, or simply apply gut instinct and feeling. If a choice is really right, it will feel absolutely true and rock-solid. If you have doubt, you will feel a sense of discomfort, tightness, and uneasiness. If past decisions evoke these feelings of uncertainty, this is a clear signal that you need to reexamine the underlying issues involved. You are getting an inner warning that something is not right.

Heed the inner voice, because it is giving you some very important information about your future. Below, jot down any major changes you want to make in your life: life mission, career, relationships, other goals. Spend a few minutes now reviewing each of these intuitively.

Major decisions to review

_____

_____

_____

_____

_____

Intuitive thinking has proven to be an important path to success for many people. Perhaps it is the right path for you, as well. Remember that your lifetime happiness and fulfillment are the sum total of all the decisions you make each day. Improve your decision-making, and you vastly improve your results. By combining intuitive thinking with rational thinking, you have all the tools you need to make important decisions with confidence. Of course, intuition is not a substitute for professional help in areas such as medicine, law, or financial matters. Unless you are a pro in such fields, it's best to heed the advice of experts. But for the many final decisions that you must make alone, first think clearly and rationally, then listen to your heart to be sure you have made the right choice. That is the way to ensure success.

Today's journal

What mattered to me today:

_____

_____

_____

_____

_____

Coincidences, hunches, breakthroughs I experienced today:

_____

_____

_____

_____

New ideas I had today:

_____

_____

_____

_____

My thoughts, feelings, reflections on today:

_____

_____

_____

_____

Plan for abundance

You can't change the wind, but you can adjust your sails.

—Tom Winninger

Welcome to the final week of the Countdown! You deserve a lot of credit, because you have come a long way and have made much progress exploring paths to personal growth and success. But there is much more to come. We are beginning a new section today on *abundance*. If your definition of success includes material and financial abundance, today and tomorrow's paths are ones to intrigue you. Today's chapter is especially important if you plan to sell or market any kind of product or service, or if you have considered starting your own business in order to achieve success.

Will the plans you make today put you in the right place tomorrow, and bring you the abundance you want and deserve? Will you be where you need to be in order to maximize results? Remember, success does not care about who you are, but it cares a lot about where you are.

163

Three sustaining forces

What does planning for abundance mean? Here's an example: Hundreds of years ago, early American settlers found that their best chance for success came when they lived and worked beside a major waterway. Of course, not everyone who settled on a waterway was guaranteed prosperity, but that body of water provided three sustaining forces: nourishment in the form of food and water, a mode of transportation, and a source of trade and commerce. Some of today's most vibrant American cities grew from those early settlements.

Plan to be in the right place

Positioning yourself for success in today's world is more complex than the pioneers' early strategy. Today you must plan to take advantage of as many factors as possible. After all, if you're going to make the effort to go for your goals, you might as well give yourself every chance of winning. It's funny that when someone achieves success, others say that person was just lucky, or happened to be in the right place at the right time. In actuality, luck is knowing what you want and placing yourself in the right place at the most propitious time. You create the design, you make the plans, you harness the internal and external forces and then bring them all together to bring your dream to fruition. That is called positioning yourself for success.

A colorful success

Loren Berry positioned himself for success. According to *Forbes* magazine, as a kid he sold products to his neighbors, learning early that the best way for him to make money was to sell things. He decided to make selling his career and realized he would have to go where the action was to make it big. In the big city he looked for a way to tap into the vast sums of money businesses spent on advertising. Noticing that companies spent money to be listed in the telephone book, he figured he could sell them ads along with those listings. Because the white paper used for phone books was so expensive, Berry tried using cheaper, yellow paper to print his telephone book ads. His idea caught on fast, and soon his business phone directories became very popular and well-known as the yellow pages. By being in the right place at the right time intentionally, Loren Berry became a millionaire many times over.

Three forces of modern prosperity

Too often, people make plans but fail to consider the factors that can bring them success or failure. Just as the settlers harnessed the river's three forces of prosperity—food, transportation, and trade—you can harness what might be considered three forces of modern prosperity: *economics, demographics,* and *psychographics.*

First, economics is simply the creation, growth, and management of wealth. In other words, economics is where money comes from and where it goes. In Loren Berry's case, he knew that lots of money was being spent by businesses to advertise. He decided he would access the flow of that vast river of money.

Second, demographics is the study of human populations: birth rates, age, sex, income levels, ethnic composition, and so on. In other words, demographics refers to people—who they are, what they are, and where they can be found. Again using the example of Loren Berry, he knew that thousands of businesses were already spending money to advertise in phone books to reach customers among the millions of people who received the phone books.

Finally, psychographics is the study of people's attitudes, opinions, and activities. It is what people think, how they act, and what they do. In Loren Berry's case, he was building his business on a common, daily activity—people who needed to find a business or service would grab the phone book to look it up. The phone book was already a well-accepted, everyday object that people everywhere used on a daily basis, and Berry capitalized on that common activity.

Position yourself for success by using the power of all these forces in your plans.

Increase your chances

Virtually every successful person who has achieved prosperity used all three of these factors to reach his or her goals. People who fail to achieve success generally overlook one or more of these three factors. A store owner who locates his store away from population centers, in an inaccessible place, is overlooking the demographic factor. Someone who provides an overpriced service or product to others, or one that is of little value is overlooking the factors of economics. And a person who plans to sell something that people rarely use may be overlooking the psychographics factor. The reality is that more than half of all new small businesses fail in the first four years. In the excitement of making plans, people focus on the excitement instead of the major forces that can make them or break them.

Some people do all right despite disregarding some of these rules, but why go into the game with the odds against you? By using all the forces of prosperity to your advantage, you can dramatically increase your chances for abundant success.

The first force: economics

Let's kick off a question-and-answer exercise to show you how to position yourself for success. Through a series of questions, you can test this path as you discover ways to adjust your plans to take maximum advantage of the economic, demographic, and psychographic forces that affect your goal.

First, if you want abundance, the economics factor is one you've probably already considered in your plans. Now is the time to consider it more carefully. Remember, economics is the creation, growth, and management of wealth. You create wealth by creating value for others, and then distributing that value to as many people as possible.

Answering economic questions

Consider the following questions as they apply to your plans to reach your goals. As you consider each question, write down a brief answer in the book.

In what way(s) does your plan to achieve prosperity offer real value *to others?*

In what way(s) does your plan for success offer specialized knowledge that is uncommon, a unique and unusual service, or a product that is not easily found elsewhere?

Are you creating something new, or enhancing something that already exists? If not, how could you?

In what way(s) will you offer others the best possible quality in your product or service?

In what way(s) can you somehow increase the value of what you plan to offer to others?

Sometimes you can improve your economic positioning just by looking at your plans a little differently. Consider your product or service with a critical eye from the consumer's point of view. See if you can make it better and more valuable. Make your marketing and sales happen from the customer's standpoint, not your own.

Change your point of view

Someone said once that Sears sold its customers a million half-inch drill bits last year, but none of their customers actually wanted drill bits. What they really wanted were half-inch holes! That is an example of taking a different point of view. Thomas Levitt said that Kodak's success came from taking the customer's perspective. He pointed out that Kodak sells film, but they don't advertise film, they advertise memories. That is a different and accurate point of view. Another person with a different point of view is beauty industry giant Charles Revson. Revson once said, "In our factory we make lipstick, but in our advertising, we sell hope." Break out of your current thinking, turn things around, look for new ways to give others what they really want, not what you think they want. Get positioned for economic success by creating real value, higher quality, and superior levels of service.

The distribution factor

As you consider the economics of your plan, consider the key factor of distribution. Ask yourself the following questions and jot down the answers.

How will you distribute your goods or services to others?

If you plan to start a business, must your customers be local only? Can you offer your product or service outside your immediate area?

In what way(s) can you access a regional, national, or worldwide base of customers?

In what way(s) can you take advantage of mass sales and distribution to get your product or service to thousands or millions of people?

If you are offering others information of some kind, in what way(s) can you use media such as video and the Internet, to offer it to many simultaneously?

A bad hair day pays off

In 1989, a woman named Tomima Edmark had difficulty getting her hair to look just right, so she created a unique but simple device to help her braid her hair. She decided that other women could benefit from her unique product. First, she came up with a name for her invention: Topsytail. She started selling it part-time without much luck. Then she talked *Glamour* magazine into running a piece on her product. Edmark told me that just three weeks after the national magazine hit the stands she had received $100,000 in orders! With that capital, she used television direct response marketing to offer the product to an even bigger national audience. In just a matter of months, she sold more than three-and-a-half million Topsytails at $15 apiece, creating significant wealth for herself.

Reprinted with special permission of King Features Syndicate.

The second force: demographics

Let's move on to the second force of prosperity: demographics. Again, demographics refers to factors such as age, sex, income level, ethnicity, and education of the population. Demographics is a statistical science, so you can easily find some reliable data regarding your particular plans for success. If you think this sounds boring, believe me, there is nothing boring about how the right demographic information can affect your results in the years ahead.

Consider the following examples of statistics and their related questions. Jot down the answers or do the research necessary to get the answers. You will find plenty of demographic information in the reference section of any library.

Age

U.S. projections on aging show, for example, that the segment of the population aged 45 to 54 will increase 44 percent by the year 2000. At the same time, the group aged 25-34 will drop by 17 percent. How will these changes, and other current age projections, affect your plans for success?

169

Income

It is important to consider changes in household incomes. During the growth decade of the 1980s, nearly the entire population's income rose after taxes. Those with the highest disposable incomes had significant salary growth during those years. And again, in the late 1990s, household incomes rose again. Will changes in disposable income affect the spending of your potential customers? Do you plan to sell an upscale product or service, or something everyone can afford? Is there a way for you to offer a product or service at a significantly lower cost than someone else?

Who are you targeting?

As you make your plans, be sure to define exactly who will be creating your prosperity. In other words, who is your target customer? You may feel your product or service is perfect for every consumer, but every product or service does better when specifically tailored to the needs of a defined, target customer. In today's world, there are very few goods or services of value that are "one-size-fits-all." Focus on the bullseye, and you will be sure to hit your target. What is the age, gender, and income of your ideal customer? Are these people in demographic growth segments? In other words, will you have more or fewer customers 10 years from now? Should you change your plans to target a wider segment of potential customers, or to superserve a narrow, more specific group of customers?

Starting a business

Drew Massey is the founder of *P.O.V.* (Point of View), a men's magazine focusing on career, money, and "living large." In a recent radio interview, Massey told me he had his "epiphany" while working for *Forbes* magazine. It suddenly hit him that there wasn't a magazine for readers like him: affluent 20-something guys. Somehow, the magazine industry had overlooked this prime demographic target. At age 25, Massey quit his job and two years later, published the first issue of his new monthly magazine to rave reviews. Today, *P.O.V.* has nearly 250,000 subscribers and a host of blue-chip advertisers, thanks to Massey's sharp focus on a key demographic target.

The third force: psychographics

Finally, consider these psychographic questions, keeping your goals in mind. Remember, psychographics is the study of people's attitudes, opinions, and activities. Attitudes are often formed in our youth, which is why different generations tend to have different outlooks.

Ann Clurman is an expert on generational marketing. She's co-author (with J. Walter Smith) of *Rocking the Ages* (HarperBusiness, 1997) and a partner with Yankelovich Partners, Inc., a leading consumer research firm. Here's how she explained the concept of marketing to generations during a broadcast interview I had with her.

> *What we mean by generational marketing is that there are groups in our population who belong to distinct generations. It goes beyond the fact that we are of a certain age. What it means is that there are experiences that happen to us when we are coming of age that shape our values and the way we look at life, and that these experiences act as a sort of generational filter through which we view those around us and things that happen to us as we continue on in life.*
>
> *It's useful to think of adults today as one of three generations. First, the Matures, who were born pretty much between 1909 and about 1945. That's the generation that licked the Depression, fought the Second World War, overcame fascism, rebuilt America, and basically began the move to the suburbs. Second, there are the Baby Boomers, born between about 1946 and 1964. That's 78 million people who grew up in a time when they assumed unending economic prosperity and that they could kind of paint the world in whatever image they wanted it to be. Third, Generation X, born between about 1965 and 1978. They grew up in the 80s, and that time included a lot of turmoil, a lot of divorce. This is the generation that learned very early not to take anything for granted.*

In general, Clurman says, different generations have different outlooks. Their widely varied views of the world mean they will not respond equally to a single approach. Clurman suggests you study the core values that your product or service represents. Then use her book or other research to determine the appeal to different generations. It is possible to market across generations, but it requires a thoughtful approach and the right product or service.

Jot down some answers to these questions.

Do you plan to market your product or service to a specific genera-tion? If so, how will they view the core values represented by your prod-uct or service?

How will people's different attitudes and opinions affect your plan?

How will people's different interests and activities affect your plan?

What's ahead?

Big companies spend lots of time and money answering questions about the future. Faith Popcorn is one of a number of so-called futur-ists who are hired by big business to make such predictions. She fore-saw a change in people's behavior, called *cocooning*: More folks stay-ing at home for meals and entertainment, rather than going out as often. This trend has affected a number of businesses, such as video stores, catalogs, and food delivery services. You can spot such changes by reading books about future trends, by being focused on new pat-terns of behavior, and just by looking at the changing interests of the people around you.

For example, you may have noticed that people have become more interested in the environment in recent years, and that the clout of the environmental movement has increased as well. Because of this, recyclers and sellers of so-called "green" products and services are riding an environmental wave of growth. Could your plan benefit from a current or future psychographic movement?

The small business market

Tom Stemberg predicted the growth of home offices and of small business when he founded Staples, the first discount office supply store, in 1986. Chances are you have shopped in a Staples store, or one like it. Today, Staples has 500 stores and annual sales of more than $3 billion. It has spawned a host of successful imitators. Tom Stemberg was in the right place at the right time. In 1989, 28 million people were working at home. By 1994, that number had grown to 40 million. Ask yourself how people's activities may change in the next five to 10 years, and how can you use these trends to your benefit.

Time is money

One trend that appears to be a safe bet is people's attitude toward time. Everyone wants to save time, because time is the one thing that money cannot buy. According to *American Demographics* magazine, less than 30 percent of American homes had microwave ovens in 1982. By 1992, more than 80 percent of homes had microwave ovens. That is incredible growth for a relatively expensive product, especially considering that the microwave oven doesn't do a great job of cooking food. It does do one thing very well—it saves time.

New businesses often seek ways to save time for their customers, and many are successful. For example, a few years back I noticed that *Success* magazine's annual review of top franchises was loaded with names such as Candy Express, Heel Quik, Check Express, and Fastsigns. Is there a way to apply the factor of time saving to your plan?

Position yourself for success

At this point, you should have some answers to questions about the economic, demographic, and psychographic forces that affect your plans. If this path resonates with you, you will want to learn all you can about these areas. You can take advantage of the three forces of prosperity and position yourself for success by putting yourself in the right place at the right time.

Today's journal

What mattered to me today:

_____

_____

_____

_____

_____

Coincidences, hunches, breakthroughs I experienced today:

_____

_____

_____

_____

New ideas I had today:

_____

_____

_____

_____

My thoughts, feelings, reflections on today:

_____

_____

_____

_____

Attract more money

There's a reason most people are poor. It's not by accident.

—Brett Machtig

If your personal path to success includes prosperity, there are some established, simple steps you should learn to follow. For many people, financial abundance is an important part of their dreams. Creating true lifelong prosperity is today's focus as you explore how successful people build wealth. By applying today's lessons you can follow a path to prosperity no matter what your present financial situation.

Wealth perceptions

Some people say it's wrong to want financial abundance, and that it's greedy or selfish to want lots of money. You must understand something very important as you begin this chapter: Achieving personal financial abundance is your absolute right as a human being,

175

should you desire it. Some may say that in order for you to become wealthy, someone else has to become poor. Some think that if you gain money and prosperity, others will have to suffer and do without. Not true! In fact, there is enough wealth available for everyone. Bill Taylor, founding editor of *Fast Company*, a business magazine, shared an impressive statistic with me recently: The percentage of millionaires in America is now growing at a rate 20 times faster than that of the population at large! Meanwhile, there are fewer Americans living in poverty than ever before.

If you earn enough money to become rich, no one else will have less. It is fine to have money, it is acceptable to make wealth a goal, and it is quite easy to maintain positive values along with prosperity. When you have wealth, you can help make great things happen for others. You can share your abundance with those in need and put your money where it will do the most good in the world for you and others.

The world is overflowing with financial abundance and you can earn your share if you want to. Every day there are about 1,000 new millionaires created in America. You can join this fast-growing group simply by following the strategies that are outlined in the pages ahead.

Before you begin, here is one more good reason to become financially independent: Researchers in Canada recently found that wealthy people tend to live longer than those who earn less. In a study of 500,000 men, those who earned the most lived longest after retirement. The exact reasons are unclear, but the conclusion is obvious. Follow wealth-building strategies and you can live longer!

Money thoughts

Remember the power of thought. Negative thoughts about any goal will block you from reaching that goal, and the same holds true for wealth. You must have a *strong positive desire to achieve abundant wealth*. Negative thoughts about wealth will sabotage your quest for financial success. Focus on having money today and start believing that you are already prosperous, to help attract wealth to you. And you must eliminate any negative perceptions about wealth starting right now. You may have some stubborn negative thoughts about money from your past. Now is the time to get those negative thoughts out of your head and cleared away forever. The best way to do this is to first write them down, so you can see them clearly.

To help start you on this first step, here are some examples of negative thoughts about money:

♦ Have you or your loved ones been angry about finances?

♦ Have you said, "I'm not made of money"?

♦ Have you said, "I never have enough money"?

♦ Have you been broke, or afraid you couldn't pay your bills?

♦ Have you felt unhappy, frustrated, and helpless over your dwindling bank balance?

These are all negative financial attitudes that can keep you from achieving wealth. Take a few minutes now to write down all the negative thoughts you have had about money.

My negative money thoughts

_____

_____

_____

_____

_____

_____

_____

By putting these thoughts on paper, you can clearly see the kind of thinking that has to be eliminated to allow a positive wealth-building state of mind to flourish. Think of this process as clearing a field choked with weeds before you plant the new seeds. You also have to be careful to keep those weeds from coming back. Reject negative money thoughts anytime they pop into your head. Simply push them away, while at the same time reaffirming your new, positive attitude toward money.

To help you get this new attitude, realize what money really is. It is a *symbol*. It's not the pieces of paper and little metal tokens that you really want. It's the value and services that the paper and metal represent! Money is a symbolic key that unlocks doors representing freedom, happiness, security, and peace of mind. These are things you want and deserve. Know that you have the power to create wealth and have all the money you will ever need flow toward you. Believe that you have the power to control money, instead of letting it control you. Keep a positive money mind-set at all times.

"Money *is* something!" With those words, best-selling author and syndicated talk show host Victor Boc began telling me about a profound law of wealth creation.

> *Money is actually an energy that you can attract into your life. Sometimes when you say that, people think, "Oh boy, that sounds like a bunch of new-age psychobabble." But there are actually forces that are at play in your life day in and day out, whether you recognize them or not. This is what is happening at the most fundamental level underneath all that you do— playing the market, buying or selling real estate, and so on.*
>
> *Everybody has either a flow of money into their life, or out of their life. Most people go through life repelling money, and that's why they have such a hard time making money and hanging on to the money they do have.*

What causes you to repel money? Boc told me that if you have an *addiction* to money, in other words if you experience an emotion-backed demand for it, you will actually end up pushing it away from you! This may be a difficult concept to grasp, but you have no doubt witnessed this same law at work in other parts of your life. For example, in romance, if you addictively chase after someone, this usually repels them from you. In business, if you desperately pursue a customer, you will probably drive them away. As in everything, the key to attracting money starts with a relaxed, positive attitude, not an attitude of addictive neediness. Victor Boc gives a step-by-step plan for prosperity in his bestseller, *How to Solve All Your Money Problems Forever* (Perigee, 1998).

Three robbers

Once you have the right attitude about money, your next step is to outwit what wealth expert and noted financial author Brett Machtig calls the *three robbers*. These robbers can steal away your ability to achieve financial independence before you even know it. Not surprisingly, these three robbers are common patterns of behavior. We have covered some of these faulty behaviors in previous chapters, but here they apply to money. Machtig described the robbers to me in a recent interview:

The first of the three robbers is procrastination. People don't start! They think that wealth is so elusive that it's not going to happen. The average person will spend 20 or 30 years working before they start the wealth building process. And I figured out why: I think at some level people believe they are going to be financially better off down the road. So they let a day pass, a week pass, and a month pass. Literally, 20 or 30 years can pass before people get the kick in the pants and say, "Today I'm going to start saving."

The second robber is debt. Debt allows people to spend money that they don't even have. So what happens is people have every single nickel going out to pay their bills. It turns out the wealthy aren't wealthy because they have large portfolios. They are wealthy because they have eliminated their biggest bills.

The third robber is ignorance—ignorance about how to invest. It's imagining that you somehow know what the future will bring and investing based on that. Typically, people put all their money into things that have just done well. And, they invest for too short a time for the money to do well. Within that short time-frame, these people don't understand how to apply the rules of risk-versus-reward to give them the highest rate of return.

Certainly you understand procrastination. And surely you know the importance of avoiding or getting out of debt. But maybe you don't recognize the third robber, which is failure to invest wisely. Most people try to chase money by investing in the newest hot mutual fund or latest trend. For example, they might buy shares of a stock that's making the news headlines, when its price is already at the top. To avoid the third robber, do not follow the usual stampede of investors. Instead, follow a smart, long-term investment strategy. And understand that the greater risk you take, the greater is the potential for reward, but your risk tolerance may vary.

Keep the images of these three robbers fixed clearly in your mind, and plan to avoid them at all costs. Do not fall victim to them as so many others have.

"Wealth in a decade"

You now know the negatives to avoid. What positive actions can you take to attract money? It's time to explore the laws of wealth creation. Yes, there really is a set of rules you can follow to become wealthy. Brett Machtig knows for certain that these laws work, that they are as dependable and consistent as the law of gravity! His book, *Wealth in a Decade* (Irwin, 1995), explains the laws that you or anyone can apply to become wealthy in just 10 short years. If this seems hard to believe, Machtig backs up his claim with plenty of examples. (None of them involve winning the lottery, either!)

The definition of wealth Machtig uses is reasonable and still exciting. It is building your investments to a point where, in 10 years, you can live off the interest earned from your investments at about the same life style level you live now. If you want to live higher, you need to save, invest, and earn more. After 10 years, if you want to quit work, change to a different profession, or keep working, you have the luxury of making that decision.

That luxury means you will be living like most millionaires. But did you know that most millionaires work at something, they don't live ostentatiously, and they're savers, not spenders? For example, despite his incredible wealth, billionaire Warren Buffett still lives in the same modest, comfortable Omaha home he has owned for many years. This kind of approach to life has helped him make billions, and it is fairly typical of the life styles of the truly rich.

Laws of wealth

Brett Machtig followed the path of learning from leaders when he set out to learn the ways to wealth. He researched many wealthy people and learned the steps they followed consistently. His laws of wealth begin with financial goal-setting.

First, calculate all your present monthly expenses. Multiply the monthly total by 12 to get how much money you need each year. This is the sum, not adjusted for inflation, that your nest egg must spin off in annual interest to provide you with financial independence. Remember, you will live off the interest only, always leaving the principal intact to generate income through wise investments.

To learn how big your total nest egg must be, divide the sum of your annual needs by 8 percent, an average rate of return. This is the target figure you must build up through savings and smart investment. With this sum well invested, your annual income needs will be fully paid for by interest alone. You never have to touch the principal itself, which guarantees you a steady income for the rest of your life.

Reprinted with special permission of King Features Syndicate.

Once you know the exact financial goal you must meet to achieve financial independence, the next steps obviously involve saving and investing your way to that number. And, yes, virtually anyone who is committed can do it in about 10 years or less.

Save your way to wealth

Frugality is an ancient, honorable, and largely forgotten concept that means practicing economy. Boiled down to its essence, to be frugal only means to spend less than you earn. It's that simple, and it's also the surest way to wealth when you add the concept of investing what you save. But it doesn't mean to go on a financial diet. Going on a financial diet sounds about as appealing as going on a strict food diet. It feels downright uncomfortable and is no fun. Bottom line: It does not work. Harsh food diets do not work and harsh money diets do not work, because we feel deprived and we get rebellious. If that weren't simple human nature, the billion-dollar diet industry wouldn't exist.

A harsh savings plans doesn't work, because it isn't psychologically rewarding. So don't plan to cut back on the occasional dinners out, or the other little luxuries that make living more fun. As Machtig emphasized to me, real savings come from cutting back the big bills, such as car payments and major travel. These big expenses can be reduced without pain or loss. In other words, postponing or minimizing major expenditures is where you will find the money for wealth! As startling as it seems, saving a few dollars here and there can really add up over time. Machtig gave me an example: Save just $1 per day for about 40 years, and at 10 percent interest you will end up with more than $200,000. Now, that's certainly painless and the result is the kind of money that puts anxiety to rest.

Pay yourself first

Every time you get money, every time you are paid, pay yourself first. Take part of the money and immediately pay down debts like credit card bills, and then put a portion of your money into your savings plan. You might set up an automatic payroll deduction plan to put money right into your savings plan every time you are paid. This makes it easy for you to avoid the temptation to spend money before it's saved. Often, paycheck withholding for a 401(k) is done before tax is deducted, which effectively increases your 401(k) contribution and lowers your tax bite.

Use the power of compounding

Compound interest is about the closest thing there is to magic in the world of money. That's where the interest earned on your savings earns even more interest. If you don't withdraw it but leave it in the savings vehicle, add to the principal, and let the process of compounding work its magic, it builds and builds and builds. Use the power of *compound interest* and *automatic reinvestment* to build your wealth.

Sure, you could save your money under the mattress, but you would actually be losing money, because the value would keep shrinking due to inflation. Investing your money makes it grow. Make sure your savings plan pays sufficient interest, and that the interest is compounded. Equally important is to be certain that your interest is automatically reinvested. This strategy will accelerate the growth of your money. Every time your money spins off some interest, it goes back into your original investment, so the total pot grows. As the years go by, your money will multiply faster and faster.

Protect yourself

An important step to financial abundance is to *protect yourself and your wealth*. For example, be sure you have a legal will to protect your loved ones. This will also guarantee that your money will go where you want it to when you die. Buy enough insurance to protect against catastrophe. Have sufficient homeowner's, health, automobile, and personal liability coverage. Without insurance, it takes just one major accident, fire, or injury to wipe out your wealth, so be sure you safeguard against catastrophe.

The final law of wealth creation

There's one more law of wealth creation, and it's an important one. I call it the *Law of Reciprocity*, and it is as old as recorded history. The essence is that you get wealth by attracting it, not by chasing it. Money is attracted to you when you provide something of value to others. The greater the value of the service you give, and the more people you give it to, the greater your financial rewards will be. The more you give, the more will flow back to you. (This path of *giving to others* is a major one, and it will be fully explored later in the Countdown.) The Law of Reciprocity is an eternal rule of wealth creation. As you take steps to attract more money, always keep this rule in mind.

Share and get rich

Money manager George Soros is a billionaire and he gives some $300 million a year to causes that he believes will make the world a better place. No doubt his generosity has helped him become so rich. The late Dr. Leo Buscaglia is a very successful author and speaker with book sales of nearly 20 million copies. He says, "The best reason to make a million dollars is so you can give it away." You needn't be a billionaire, or even a millionaire, to make this law work for you.

Whenever you make money, share a little of your financial abundance with others. Begin sharing at least 1 percent (but no more than 5 percent) of your after-tax income with others today. If you do not think you have enough money for yourself now, remember that the more you give to others, the more will flow back to you. How can this happen? At a higher level of your being, the act of giving sends out a powerful message of abundance and plenty. This abundance then flows back to you. It is as basic as breathing. You breath in oxygen, which you need, and you exhale carbon dioxide, which green, growing things need. There is a continuous give-and-take process happening here. Stop one part of the process and you die. The same holds true for money. Consistently give some money back, and money will keep flowing toward you. It is a very important part of the wealth mind-set you need to succeed. Share with others and put reciprocity to work for you. One caveat on financial balance: It is possible to give away too much! Give to others what you can afford to give, without harshly depriving yourself.

Remember, your wealth is a measure of how much you have saved, served, and given to others. Abundant wealth is the right of everyone willing to earn it. If the path of financial abundance is one that resonates with you, follow the steps outlined in this chapter starting today, and you will soon attract more money.

Today's journal

What mattered to me today:

_____

_____

_____

_____

_____

Coincidences, hunches, breakthroughs I experienced today:

_____

_____

_____

_____

_____

New ideas I had today:

_____

_____

_____

_____

_____

My thoughts, feelings, reflections on today:

_____

_____

_____

_____

_____

Focus your mind

There is nothing that the human mind cannot do.

—Jose Silva

In the final five days of the Countdown, you will explore some of the most powerful paths to success used by top achievers. I hope you have been examining each of the different routes to success presented over the last 16 days, carefully evaluating each approach to see if it resonates for you. Along the way you have crossed a few of the five final paths. Now you will have the chance to explore them fully.

It's worth noting here that some of these ideas may challenge your belief system and require you to suspend your doubts. You will be asked to surrender to the idea that these paths may be right for you. Your rational left brain might tell you that some of these concepts seem farfetched or completely impossible. Of course, radio and television, manned spacecraft, computers, biotechnology, and countless other inventions and discoveries were considered impossible fantasies just 100 years ago. Today, they are facts of life. Maybe your spacecraft is just ahead.

"You can't teach an old dog new tricks." While that saying has been disproved in some cases, it is probably more true of humans. Most people's thinking and belief systems get locked in place by the time they are a certain age. Once set, these systems tend not to change and this rigidity can be limiting. But if you can change your thinking, you can change your life. It takes courage, because few have what it takes to throw out safe, comfortable, old ways of thinking and try something new.

Open your mind to new ideas, starting today, and you can open the door to seemingly unbelievable levels of success.

Mental "channel surfers"

Your thoughts create your reality. What kind of thinker are you? Many people go through the day like a channel surfer, endlessly flipping past countless TV channels, never staying with one for long. A channel surfer repeatedly punches the remote control, getting only a brief image here or a quick phrase there, gathering little more than wasted time. Likewise, one whose mind flits from one mental image to the next, with his inner voice chattering endlessly and a constant stream of thoughts passing through his head never has the chance to harness the full power of his mind.

It is estimated that most people only use 10 to 15 percent of their brain's total capacity during their lifetime. Yet nature is not wasteful. This capacity exists for a reason. Part of this normally unused realm can be used to achieve high levels of concentration. When you learn how to scientifically focus your mind, you begin to tap previously unused brain power.

Brain waves

Jose Silva has always been fascinated by the human mind. His career was in electronics, but his interest in the human mind and how it works led him to perform research in this field. Later on, his young children's poor grades in school made him wonder if hypnosis or another mental technique might improve their ability to learn. For nine years, he tried mental training on his own children, and as he refined his techniques, the kids made remarkable progress in their school work and in many other areas of their lives.

From his electronics background, Silva knew that the human mind works with its own electricity. Prior research by others had revealed that the brain emits electrical waves at different rates. The slowest of these, *delta* and *theta* waves, at one to seven cycles per second, occur during sleep. The fastest, *beta* waves, more than 14 cycles per second, happen during full consciousness. There is one more level of brain activity, alpha waves, which to Silva seemed the most promising of all. The alpha state occurs when the brain is between sleep and wakefulness, seven to 14 cycles per second. Alpha waves occur naturally immediately before or after slumber, in that time of twilight thought when sudden inspiration or clear insight happens. Unlike when you are fully awake, in the alpha state your mind is free to soar. You have probably experienced this when you are drowsing in bed, just before or after sleep, or while relaxing in a meditative state.

Alpha waves

Silva followed his scientific research on alpha-level training for many more years, working with adults and children. He discovered a simple way for people to reach the alpha state, and then developed a set of visualization techniques to apply at that level. Eventually, he created a program called the Silva Method to teach these skills to others. Since that time, millions of people around the world have received the Silva training. I've taken several Silva training courses and recommend them as an effective tool to focus your mind to improve many areas of your life, including your health, relationships, career, and more.

The alpha state offers a scientific way to access the benefits of a focused mind. Recently I spoke with Jose Silva during a brief break in his world travels. During our conversation, I asked him about his technique. Here's what Silva had to say:

[The Silva Method] involves making your mind function actively, and by that I mean deductively, at a specific brain frequency.

The brain functions at four different brain frequencies, delta, theta, alpha, and beta. There are two different places where the brain can become resonant and become aware. These are in beta or in alpha.

To be able to function at alpha, we need to deepen our awareness with relaxation exercises. Once we arrive at that brain frequency, we can then learn to actively function deductively there.

Silva says that this practice at the alpha level can allow us to tap into unused portions of the brain.

We can learn to use our left brain to detect information, and the right brain to transmit information. In other words, the left brain should be used for action and the right brain should be used for thinking. Ninety percent of humanity use only the left brain for both thinking and acting. It's saturated!

Remember when AM radio was in existence, before FM? The band was so loaded they had to turn off some [AM] transmitters at night to allow others to come on, because they didn't have enough room. Then they discovered FM. Now we have a new, different band for communication and even better quality. The same thing's happening with the human brain. We are saturating the left brain like AM, and the right brain is not being used!

Only 10 percent of humanity are using the brain correctly, and the rest need to be taught how to use it.

Finally, Jose Silva explained to me the reason he considers the right brain to be such an unlimited, powerful resource for achievement:

Each of our brain hemispheres has a set of senses. The left one has the biological senses, and the right one the subjective senses. We have two sets of senses being recorded, but we are not using the information being recorded in the right because it is called the subconscious. So what we are doing [in alpha] is opening the subconscious.... All we need to solve our problems is information. And we have lots of information in the subconscious to solve any kind of problem!

It's all natural

You may be skeptical or even suspicious of any technique that involves changing the frequency of your brain waves in order to access the subconscious mind. But the fact is, the alpha state is perfectly natural. As already stated, your adult mind automatically enters this state when you cross the threshold into or out of sleep. Also, scientists tell us that the minds of young children always function at the alpha level, awake or asleep. It is only when humans reach their early teens that they start to lose this natural quality. From that age and on through adulthood, our minds typically remain at the beta level during waking hours.

Perhaps the fact that kids are always in the alpha state helps explain their natural creativity and direct, often profound, wisdom. These qualities are all too often lost when we reach adulthood. This is not to say that being at the alpha level will make you childlike, but it can let you access a level of creative thinking and mental focus you might not otherwise experience as an adult. It can help you analyze information in new and different ways, help you bring back forgotten facts, and vastly improve your intuitive skills.

Such rewards require a dedicated approach. You can learn about the Silva Method from the best-selling book *The Silva Method of Mind Control* (Pocket Books, 1982), or better yet, by taking a weekend course from a trained Silva instructor. Classes are offered regularly in most major cities around the world. While not inexpensive, graduates get to take the basic course as often as they wish for the rest of their life, free of charge. And the investment in learning to focus your mind can obviously pay off in many valuable ways.

How you do it

The two keys to reach the alpha level involve calming your body, and then calming your mind, in that order. Appropriately enough for this book, you can use a simple numerical countdown to enter the alpha state. The first time you try, it takes many minutes. But with practice, you can reach the alpha state in 30 seconds or less. Once you are completely relaxed in body and mind, you use dynamic visualization to access the subconscious, projecting vivid images on your mental screen. When you are at this level, you can explore a single problem or challenge, ask a question and await an answer, or simply tune in to your deepest thoughts. You can look at your mental screen and let pictures appear on their own. You can call up images of events, objects, or people and get new perceptions of them. You can even access seemingly forgotten facts from your memory, just as you might open a file drawer to review the contents. Your mind is fully capable of all these feats right now, but you cannot make it do these things at the normal, waking beta level. Only when you are in the alpha state does it all become possible. There are many amazing stories of people who have used these techniques to do seemingly impossible things.

Focus rituals and routines

Getting to the alpha level is a great way to focus your mind, but there are other ways to get focused through the use of rituals. Repeating these rituals can calm your mind anytime and allow you to concentrate on the matter at hand. Successful people use rituals and routines to get themselves focused. Here are five of them that you can start using today.

1. Eliminate distractions. The first and most basic focus ritual is to consciously *eliminate distractions* that keep you from focusing on your goals. A simple example of such a distraction would be a constantly ringing phone. Disconnect it, get an answering machine, or get away from it. If you cannot eliminate distractions where you live or work, then go somewhere else. Find a quiet place where you can focus on your goals.

2. Feed your mind. A second focus ritual is to constantly *feed your mind stimuli* that keep you thinking of your goal. Tape up photos or other visual representations of your goals so you see them constantly. Clip pictures from magazines or even draw sketches that illustrate your desired results. Keep reviewing your goals and deadlines, and your step-by-step plans to achieve them. To stay inspired to achieve your goals listen to the audiotape version of this book (available from Harmony House at 800-743-1988). In short, keep feeding your mind positive stimulation to stay focused on the success you want to achieve.

3. Mini-rituals. A third idea is to develop what I call *mini-rituals*, seemingly insignificant routines that successful people use to get themselves into a focused state of mind. Watch any professional athlete getting ready to perform. Whether it's a tennis player about to serve, a baseball player about to swing, or a golfer about to tee off, every athlete has a personal mini-ritual of body movements and gestures to help him or her focus. Even if your mini-ritual is as simple as making a cup of coffee and turning on some classical music, develop a set routine that gets you ready to focus on your goals. Find one for yourself. Make it a set routine. Soon you will find that just performing the mini-ritual can get you focused in almost any situation.

4. Quick reflection. The fourth ritual to create focus is to *reflect quietly for a few minutes each day about your goal* and what it means to you. Just take a few moments to close your eyes in silence and picture your goal and experience it as if it was already there. Deep meditation is an even more powerful way to focus your mind on what you want in your life, and you will explore this path more fully a few days from now.

5. Take a break. The fifth focus ritual is no ritual at all! It's one to use when your mind absolutely refuses to focus on a goal: Simply take a break. On certain days, for whatever reason, you might find it very difficult to get focused. Do your usual rituals and routines and if your mind still will not cooperate, don't let it bother you. As long as you have made a real effort, do not try to force it.

Improve your mental focus today

Discover some ways now in which you can improve your mental focus. List five steps to improve your focus on your goals. Once you have completed your list, put these focus-generating ideas into action.

5 steps to improve my mental focus

1. _____

2. _____

3. _____

4. _____

5. _____

What do you notice?

A nature expert is walking with a friend along a busy downtown street. The street is jammed with noisy, honking cars and trucks. Suddenly the expert stops in his tracks and cocks his ear. He remarks to his companion how unusual it is to hear a cricket at that particular time of year. His friend is amazed and asks how he can possibly hear a cricket over the roar of the traffic. The nature expert smiles, reaches into his pocket, takes out a dime and drops it on the sidewalk. As the coin hits the cement, a dozen pedestrian's heads spin around, and several of them glance down looking for the coin. The man explains to his friend that people notice the things they focus their minds on.

Certain people just seem to keep succeeding in life. Their ability to *focus on what they want* is a major reason for their continuing success. Once they get focused on a goal, their mind starts recognizing opportunities others might overlook. Likewise, there are opportunities you can take advantage of, which are just waiting for you to discover them. But unless you *keep focused* on what you want, your mind will not recognize these opportunities for success.

Today's journal

What mattered to me today:

_____

_____

_____

_____

_____

Coincidences, hunches, breakthroughs I experienced today:

_____

_____

_____

_____

New ideas I had today:

_____

_____

_____

_____

My thoughts, feelings, reflections on today:

_____

_____

_____

_____

Make a real change

Rather than focus on the negative aspect of change, which is loss,
I focus on the adventure of it and say, "What's next?"

Dennis Wholey

Since you began this program of exploration 17 days ago, you have spent a lot of time learning how to change how you think about yourself and your future. Of course, the primary path for achievement and success is found in the thoughts you focus on each day. Change your thoughts and you can literally change your life.

Making changes involves elements of risk, fear, visualization, goal-setting, and many of the other paths you've explored. But for some, change itself may prove to be the most powerful path to follow. If you dream of success but feel stuck in a limiting situation, in addictive behavior, or simply in a comfort zone, change is a path you should explore. Today, you can discover whether change itself is your best pathway to success.

What to change

There are different ways you can change. The most significant changes you can make are personal and physical, involving your behavior, your relationships, your job, and so on. Personal changes can be challenging, but in the end they can be vastly beneficial. Personal changes can move you from feeling stuck to an entirely new level of satisfaction and fulfillment. Physical changes are usually less challenging than personal changes, but they, too, can have immediate positive benefits. You will learn steps to make both personal and physical changes in your life starting today.

ZIGGY © ZIGGY AND FRIENDS, INC. Dist. by UNIVERSAL PRESS SYNDICATE. Reprinted with permission. All rights reserved.

Personal changes

You have already experienced many personal changes during your life. From the day you were born change has been constant. People entered your life and departed. You went from grade school, to high school, to college, and beyond. Relationships began and ended. You probably changed jobs. You probably picked up new habits and dropped old ones.

Children accept and adjust to changes more easily than adults. That's partly because changes come less quickly as we grow older. Life becomes more predictable and we settle into a rhythm. Then, when change pops up, we tend to resist it—even when change is the best thing that can happen to us.

If you find that making a necessary change is a struggle, and that fear or inability to change holds you back, you must step back and revise your tactics. A change of attitude will benefit you. You need to adopt a healthier attitude, one that welcomes change. Once you do, you will understand that while the process involves a form of loss, it also brings benefits that you will enjoy. One day another change will be required. That's an inevitable part of living.

Change means loss

Dennis Wholey is a PBS host, a recovering alcoholic, and a best-selling author of several books on change. His first book, *The Courage to Change* (Warner Books, 1994), has become a positive resource for alcoholics and their families. After writing it, Dennis realized that readers who wanted to change themselves in ways unrelated to alcohol were also drawn to the book. That led him to write *The Miracle of Change* (Pocket Books, 1997), in which he offers the insights of many wise people who made difficult but important life changes. In virtually every case, these changes opened the way to self-discovery and growth. In a candid interview, Dennis Wholey spoke with me about how personal change can benefit anyone, despite the feeling of loss.

> *Change is always in the air, and as human beings we are always having to deal with it. It doesn't make any difference if it's a change that is thrust upon us—changes that happen from the outside in—such as when a parent dies, a relationship ends, or a company downsizes, or change that we try to make happen ourselves: we move to a new city, get a new job, or quit smoking. It's all part of the way life works.*
>
> *Many times, change has to do with loss. Anytime there is any loss in our lives, whether it's a parent, friend, a spouse, a partner, a job, or anything that we love, there is going to be a lot*

of anguish and discomfort, and a lot of fear kicks in. All of us have to learn to deal with these big hits in life. The plus side is these big hits teach us about loving ourselves and other people unconditionally, developing an appreciation for life, and ultimately making a close relationship with God. So change, rather than being bad because we lose things, is really a good thing because it gets us closer to the goal we all want, which is to be happy.

Dennis Wholey told me that change requires us to get out of our comfort zone. This can be hard to do, but there is a big payoff when we do decide to go for it:

How can you stay in that job when you're dragging yourself to work every day? How can you stay in that relationship that's so abusive? But coming out the other side, you look back and say, "I'm so much more free to be myself nowadays. How could I have invested that much in that relationship? How could I have let that person have such a hold on me? Or, thank God that company downsized, so I was let go!" You often hear people in their 40s or 50s say that they had invested so much in a career that had nothing to do with who they really were, but had to do only with the business of making money.

I look back on the day I wandered in to see this priest who ran a treatment center for alcoholics and drug addicts, and I put my life on the table. The anger, the worry, the depression, the self-pity, the thoughts of suicide, the fear that ran my life! And I look at my life today: five books, five national television shows, terrific friends, good relationships, a few bucks in the bank...a lot of success.

Rather than focus on the negative aspect of change, which is loss, I focus on the adventure of it and say, "What's next?"

The comfort zone trap

Instinctively you know that change can be very positive. You may have promised yourself that you're going to make some important changes in your life for very positive reasons. Maybe you want to quit a compulsive behavior, start a new career, end a relationship or start a new one, or begin a healthy diet. If so, why haven't you made these changes? Probably because you are trapped inside a comfort zone.

Most of us would rather continue to deal with familiar pain than risk unfamiliar pain outside this zone. "The Circle of Fear" is what Wholey calls the line that separates the comfort zone from where you must go to change. Obviously, this name describes how you feel when you step over the line. Fear and anxiety aren't always obvious, he told me, but sometimes sneak out of your subconscious mind and manifest themselves in hidden ways: aches and pains, grouchiness, bad dreams, and so on. This is your body telling you what your mind is feeling, and it can hurt a lot. However, you don't have to stay stuck; you have a choice. You can either step outside your comfort zone and live with these manifestations, or you can work to expand your comfort zone to encompass the area of change.

Generally, once you make the change and realize that life simply goes on, your comfort zone will automatically expand to include this new area. This shows personal growth, which is what has allowed your comfort zone to get bigger.

Expand your zone

Even before your comfort zone enlarges, before you make that difficult change that you know will be for the best, what can you do to expand your zone? How can you make tough changes easier? One way is to look at change the way you look at any risk, and apply the techniques you learned on Day 13: How to take risks with confidence. Prepare, visualize, and rehearse mentally for the change you are going to make, and then make it. Also, apply the other techniques you have learned from these pages, such as affirmations, mental focus, and goal-setting.

Reach out

Another way to manage change is to ask someone to assist you. Alcoholics can turn to Alcoholics Anonymous. Gamblers can lean on

Gamblers Anonymous. There are people available to help you change addictive behaviors of all kinds, and they're as close as your telephone.

Therapists can be an enormous help when you're wrestling with personal change. Psychotherapy is now accepted by most people as readily as any other professional care. At one point in my life when I was having trouble making a necessary change, therapy was of great value to me. A therapist has an objective viewpoint, which is invaluable when you are in the midst of a personal struggle with change. Talking with close and trusted friends can also help you. Friends can support your persistence in sticking with a difficult change when you are outside your comfort zone.

Finally, one of the most powerful ways to make a major change in your life is with regular meditation. Accessing your higher self through meditation taps into a hidden power source. This inner strength, whether you consider it spiritual or not, can help ease you through the most painful changes. Prayer, visits with clergy, and attending religious services are other ways to help you survive and thrive through change.

Personal change is a powerful path that can be life-transforming. From the loss and pain of major change you can cross new thresholds and discover greater joy than you have ever known. If this path is one you know is right for you, have the courage to follow it, starting today.

Physical change

Let's turn from personal change to physical change. Physical change is relatively easy to manage and it can help you accomplish personal change, because it's a powerful way to affect positive thoughts each day. You can create a more focused and success-oriented state of mind simply by making positive physical changes in yourself and your surroundings. Successful people do this on an ongoing basis to enhance their state of mind and improve their performance. You will get the same results by making these changes in your own life.

How can physical change have such profound effects on your state of mind? Consider, for example, how two different physical places might affect you. First, imagine you are in a gray, windowless room lit by harsh fluorescent lights. Not too motivating, is it? Next, picture yourself standing in a sunlit, fragrant pine forest high in the Colorado Rocky Mountains. Such an inspiring place would probably make your state of mind far more positive than it would be were you trapped in that gray, windowless room.

Powerful associations

You may be thinking that since inspiration, motivation, and focus come from within you, it shouldn't matter what your surroundings are. It is true that your states of mind are self-generated. But your mind constantly makes powerful associations that directly affect your thoughts and feelings. If you are in an inspiring place, your mind will naturally associate your surroundings with inspiring thoughts and emotions. If you are in a depressing place, your mind will naturally associate that place with depressing thoughts and feelings. Your mind constantly makes these powerful associations as it receives input from your physical surroundings. While you *can* feel positive almost anywhere, you will find it easier to maintain a powerfully positive state of mind with the right surroundings. Most successful people instinctively understand this connection, and use it to their advantage.

You don't have to climb to the top of the Rocky Mountains, or even leave your home, to unlock the power of physical change. Even if present circumstances force you to live in fairly dismal surroundings, you can still find ways to command the power of physical change to positively affect your thoughts.

First: change your surroundings

It is easy to start taking advantage of the power of physical change to change your state of mind. The first step is to make changes in your environment to reflect your future goals of success. You probably plan to improve your present surroundings once you start achieving your ultimate goals. You can begin taking small steps in that direction, starting today, to help reinforce your belief in future success.

Change your home

Are there any positive, visible signs in your house or apartment that reflect your dreams of the future? Is there any indication that the person who lives there (you) is reaching for success? Imagine that ideal home you have been visualizing, the one you will have in your future life. How can you affordably make some changes in your home today to start moving in that direction? Keep in mind that any positive changes you make, no matter how subtle, will provide positive reinforcement of your goals. For example, you might reduce clutter by getting rid of unneeded things, hang a new picture on the wall, have some favorite photos framed, freshen things up with a new coat of paint, repair a leaky faucet, or hire someone to do weekly cleaning.

Do not spend more money than you can afford. The goal is to make a few ongoing changes in your home that clearly indicate to you that your life is getting better. These changes will reinforce a state of mind of positive, forward momentum.

Change your work space

Does your work space or office have the look of someone who is confident about achieving success? I have walked into some executive's offices and seen pictures on the floor waiting to be hung, or half-unpacked boxes crowding the corners. These unfinished projects can begin to reflect the resident's uncertainty or indecision. Think success! If your workplace contains anything that is gathering dust in the corners (beside your co-workers), put it away or get rid of it and project the image of a winner to yourself and to others. Now it's your turn to write down five physical changes you can make to your surroundings.

5 physical changes to my surroundings

1. _____
2. _____
3. _____
4. _____
5. _____

Second: change yourself

The second step to taking advantage of the power of physical change is to change yourself physically. Look at yourself in the mirror right now and ask your image if you would look any different if you were highly successful right now, and how? If you think you would look different, why wait to make the changes? Start now.

Consider your wardrobe. Is it out of fashion or worn out? You do not have to change your whole wardrobe, but maybe you can afford a new piece once in a while. When you buy something, invest in the best quality you can afford (go to discount places and buy the best quality they have), because good clothes last longer and look better. Wayne Root, author of *The Joy of Failure* (Summit Publishing, 1996), calls this "The Armani Principle." Root cites scientific studies that show that others judge you by how you look. It is a fact of life, and it is why school kids have dress codes, executives wear suits, and police officers wear uniforms. Your clothing projects an image and covers most of your body, so why not project a success image that affects how others relate to you, and how you feel about yourself?

Check the details

As the saying goes, cleanliness is next to godliness. Consider your personal grooming. Does it reflect the look of success? Seriously take inventory of your personal grooming. Just as one's thinking can get stuck, sometimes we get used to the way we look and overlook areas for improvement. Review this critical area and be sure you look your best at all times. What about your posture? Stand tall with your spine straight. Walk like the confident winner you are. If you are overweight or out of shape, check with your doctor to make sure you are in good health, then begin to lose the pounds and firm your muscles. Make your body a physical reflection of your success state of mind, starting today. (Weight loss and exercise may fall into the personal change category for you.) Does your speech (grammar, diction, and vocabulary) reflect your success attitude? Why wait for success to arrive before you start improving these important things? Buy a book or a tape, or take a course, and make a positive change in how you speak. You might even consider investing in other positive physical changes, such as cosmetic dental work, new eyeglasses or contact lenses, and so on. Not only will you look better to others, but you will be boosting your self-confidence and success state of mind.

Now, write down five steps you could take, starting today, to make positive changes in your physical appearance.

5 physical changes to make in myself

1. _____
2. _____
3. _____
4. _____
5. _____

Third: change your location

The third way to put the power of physical change to work for you is to spend time in places that evoke powerful, positive feelings in you. Take some time on a regular basis to escape your daily environment and seek out inspiring places to visit. In an earlier example, I mentioned the Colorado Rockies. That's certainly a great place, but anyone can find equally inspiring places close to home.

Spiritual reflection

In any city or town, there are houses of worship you can visit for a time of spiritual reflection and enlightenment to help renew your positive state of mind. Even if you are not a particularly religious person, these are excellent places for quiet, thoughtful reflection. Two magnificent structures that have recharged my feelings of positive inspiration in the past are St. Patrick's Cathedral on Fifth Avenue in New York City and, not far from there, Temple Emanuel. Both are impressive structures that hold the spiritual vibrations of decades of devout prayer. No matter how stressed out you may be, you clearly sense God's presence in such places the moment you walk through the door. Let inspiring places such as these help you replace your stress and anxiety with peace and spiritual strength.

Go somewhere

No matter where you live, there are powerful places you can visit to renew your determination to succeed. Some outdoor examples include parks, open vistas, nature centers, aquariums, fountains, river walks, and lake fronts. Some indoor examples are museums, art galleries, concert halls, even the observation decks of skyscrapers. These are places you can visit on your own to get a wider perspective of the world, and focus on your personal goals of success. Plan your visits for the quietest times possible and avoid crowds. Use the power of these physical places to enhance your state of mind.

Take a moment now to write down five physical locations you can visit soon that will help you renew yourself, and give you more positive and inspired thoughts.

5 physical locations to visit

1. _____
2. _____
3. _____
4. _____
5. _____

Explore the path of change. Make the decision to go for a meaningful personal change in your life. Use the power of physical change in your home and work environment, in your personal appearance, and in the places you visit to positively impact your thoughts every day.

Today's journal

What mattered to me today:

_____

_____

_____

_____

_____

Coincidences, hunches, breakthroughs I experienced today:

_____

_____

_____

_____

New ideas I had today:

_____

_____

_____

_____

My thoughts, feelings, reflections on today:

_____

_____

_____

_____

Give others your best

Behold! I do not give lectures on a little charity.
When I give, I give myself.

—Walt Whitman

If your definition of success includes experiencing the best that life has to offer, then you will want to explore carefully today's path of giving your best to others. This is a path that includes the Law of Reciprocity, which you briefly covered as part of wealth building. Today, you can test this path of giving in all areas of life. Giving your best to others is truly a major path to success in its own right, and deserves a full day of exploration. "Give and ye shall receive" is a central law in most religions and cultures. From the Bible we are familiar with "As you sow, so shall you reap." Some Eastern religions refer to it as the Law of Karma. "You don't get something for nothing" and "There's no such thing as a free lunch" are American variations on the same theme.

What's in it for me?

Those who have limited results in their relationships, careers, family life, finances, spirituality, and other aspects of their existence probably approach these things from a position of *need*. During each encounter they want to know what's in it for them. In business transactions, they scrutinize their own bottom line and expect to see themselves coming out ahead of the other guy. In relationships they give love or friendship only when it's reciprocated. In their job they only do the work they are paid to do, and no more. Even in their relationship with God they say prayers only when their need is urgent!

Selfish patterns usually are established in childhood and by adulthood are hardened into habit. When people feel deficient or deprived, they tend to want to grab all they can and get the best of others. That may get results in the short run, but inevitably it leads to failure, disappointment, and heartache. In trying to serve yourself alone, you interrupt the natural flow of abundance that flows to all people.

On the other hand, people who give generously of themselves in relationships, in business, and in all other dealings ensure their long-term success. Friends, money, love, and even spiritual blessings arrive in abundance for the person who devotes herself to the needs of others. Is this an idealistic approach that makes no sense in big business? I posed this question to David Maister, a highly successful consultant to many top corporations and author of *True Professionalism* (Free Press, 1997), a best-selling guide to excellence in business. He replied:

> *If you do the right thing, if you do the principled thing, then the money will follow. And the good news is that if we treat others the way we want to be treated, then indeed that's the way to make money. So figure out your principles and never compromise them knowingly!*

Maister "walks his talk." When his business was still new, he completed a project for a client and realized it could have been done better. To redo the work would cost him $15,000, and it was doubtful the customer would even notice the difference. Nevertheless, he had committed himself from the start to give his clients his very best work, so he spent the money to make things right. Now he says that decision not only helped him win in the end, but gave him an unexpected dividend. His new employees saw it as a shining example of the fledgling company's commitment to excellence, and their increased motivation and performance has since paid him back many times over.

Super service

No matter what your career or field of interest, you can find ways to serve others. In business, many successful people believe that value can be summed up in these two words: *great service.* Great service has created some of the world's great fortunes. You can create vast abundance in your life as well by consistently giving your best to others. Do this and the world will seek you out and make you prosper.

I'm sure you have encountered people who were busy creating their future prosperity. They are easy to recognize, because they are the ones consistently providing extraordinary levels of service to others. Although I've probably taken a thousand cab rides, I clearly remember the occasion I climbed into a sparklingly clean taxi with a remarkably pleasant driver who made my trip a marvelous experience. I gave that driver a significantly larger tip than usual because of the great service.

There is generally a direct correlation between levels of service and financial reward. Waiters and waitresses who provide truly great service often receive larger tips than is typical. Salespeople who provide great service to their clients are usually rewarded with larger orders than other salespeople. Of course, there are exceptions to every rule. But most of the time, giving more to others results in a greater return for you.

Bill Marriott, Chairman and CEO of Marriott International, told my radio listeners that service is the secret behind his company's great success.

It's important to listen to your employees, and it's important to listen to your customers. If you want to know how to build your business, ask your customers what products they need. Ask what products they would like to have that you might be able to provide them. Do a better job of continuously improving the service to your customers!

Just how successful is Marriott International? The company's annual sales are more than $10 billion and it's now the 16th largest employer in the United States. Not bad, considering the company began as a root beer stand owned by Bill Marriott's grandfather, J. Willard Marriott. The story of this company's growth through great service is detailed in *The Spirit to Serve* (HarperBusiness, 1997) by Bill Marriott.

Excellence on wheels

People who provide excellent service are remembered, because excellence is rare. At the end of the great taxi ride I described earlier, I asked the driver why he made the extra effort. He said it was good for business—that people like to step into a clean cab, so he kept his spotless. He recognized that each of his customers had different needs, so he tried to accommodate each of them as well as he could. He said that he had tried to imagine the perfect cab-riding experience, and then made up his mind to give that experience to every single passenger, even if it was only a short ride. During my ride, for example, he asked me if I wanted to hear music, and what kind of music I liked. Then he set the radio according to my taste, without making a big deal out of it. He offered me a newspaper to read, and asked if the air felt too warm or cold. He did it all with a smile and sincerity.

Was it worth it for the driver to make this extra effort? I would say yes. First, his tips from customers were probably larger than average. I certainly gave him a very healthy tip and felt good doing it. Second, he obviously enjoyed the positive comments he received about his work, as anyone would. Clearly he took pride in what he did for a living. So his great service gave him both financial and psychological rewards, which seem well worth the few extra minutes it took during each fare.

Opportunity awaits

Because great service is worth so much to others, there's opportunity to be found where service is poor. One man discovered such an opportunity the day he took his young daughters to an amusement park. He was disappointed, because the rides were tacky and cheap looking, and the park employees rude and unfriendly. He recognized the need for a better family amusement park, one that would provide higher levels of quality and service. Potential investors didn't understand his vision. But finally the dreamer found financial backing and his park was built. Even after the doors opened he continued refining things, reaching for his vision of the perfect customer experience. One subtle change was to refer to customers as *guests*, and employees as *cast members*. You have no doubt guessed who this man is: Walt Disney. He named his park Disneyland.

Disneyland's success led to new theme parks in Florida and overseas. Disney World in Florida has become the number-one tourist destination in the world. All this prosperity came from one family's bad experience at an amusement park. Remember this story the next time you suffer because of poor service. You may have discovered an incredible opportunity.

Four steps to giving your best

By studying successful people, you will see that all great service has certain things in common. There are four steps you can follow on this path of giving your best to others.

Step one: envision the perfect experience

Allow yourself to think in the most visionary manner. Imagine that anything is possible. David Maister envisioned a perfect customer project, and realized that his initial effort fell short. That's when he decided he had to do better, even though it would cost him a small fortune. Put yourself in the position of the person being served and seek perfection in everything. When your inner voice says things like, "I can't do that," or "It's not possible," your thinking has become too limited. Open your mind to every possibility. When you imagine the perfect experience with an open mind, that's when great breakthroughs in giving will happen.

- ◆ My cab driver had envisioned the perfect cab riding experience. This gave him the knowledge he needed to make it happen.

- ◆ Walt Disney envisioned the perfect amusement park experience, far beyond anything that existed. When you visit Disney's Magic Kingdom, you will see a sparkling clean park with perfect landscaping, a graceful, soaring castle surrounded by imaginative rides, and smiling people eager to provide service. Disney imagined it and made it happen.

- ◆ Fred Smith, founder of Federal Express, envisioned the perfect delivery service experience: guaranteed overnight delivery of a package anywhere in America. It had never been done on such a scale, but Smith saw it in his mind's eye.

Allow yourself the freedom of thought to envision the perfect customer experience, and then make it happen.

Step two: get close to those you serve

Listen to those to whom you want to give. In business they are your customers; in a relationship, it is your partner; in your career, it is your boss and a co-workers. Ask them questions and respect their answers. Give recognition and attention. Acknowledge any feedback or communication you get. Encourage regular dialogue. Welcome their complaints and criticism, no matter how trivial or undeserved they seem, because you can learn a lot about how to do better. Discover the exact role you play in their lives. How could you become more important to them?

During Disney theme park training, new employees learn that most families consider a Disney World vacation the realization of a lifetime dream. In fact, some families must save for years to afford such a vacation. With this in mind, theme park workers are far more motivated to make every moment special for their visitors. After all, no one wants to spoil someone's lifetime dream! The service you offer may not fulfill a dream, but take time anyway to learn all you can about the role you play for those you serve so you can provide the best service possible.

Here's another example. The Air Force instituted a policy that requires everyone who packs parachutes to make regular jumps wearing randomly selected chutes. Now the Air Force has virtually flawless parachute-packing quality. Understand those you serve, and you will give them your best service.

Step three: go beyond the golden rule

Treat others as you want to be treated. That is the Golden Rule. Give good service, respect, honesty, fairness, patience, individual attention, and quality. Then go beyond the Golden Rule to give extraordinary levels of service, better that you personally would ever expect to receive.

Mark Victor Hansen and Jack Canfield didn't just create a series of books that motivate. They took things one step further by giving a portion of each book's profits to charity.

There are hundreds of book superstores across the country—giant, modern, multi-level places stocked with hundreds of thousands of books, and with well-trained, attentive staff to help customers find what they're looking for. Most people assume that superstores provide the highest possible level of service. But according to *Advertising Age* magazine, a woman in Denver, Colorado, reached for an even higher standard. Joyce Meskis created a book superstore with truly extraordinary customer service. Some of the features at her remarkable store include large, comfortable easy chairs throughout every department, where shoppers are invited to relax and read at their leisure. Every customer is also assumed to be trustworthy: When a customer pays by check, regardless of the amount, they are never asked for personal identification. Store employees are highly trained to make the customer's experience the best it can possibly be. These high standards of service have resulted in high customer loyalty. During a store expansion, several customers even volunteered to help move boxes!

Step four: serve others with passion

It is easy to understand this concept if you are in a strong relationship. Heartfelt giving of yourself to the other person is a basic tenet of romance. But what about in business or finance? Here, passionate service means living and breathing this attitude at all times. If you are a leader, encourage passion and heartfelt giving from those you lead, through your own constant examples. In your career, take your work to heart. Serve others with passion. If you cannot feel passionate about your work, it's time to reconsider your career!

The moment you start taking your performance for granted is the moment you start sliding. Keep tinkering and improving, keep observing and learning. Create a written work ethic or mission statement for yourself that is short and powerful and that reflects your pride in and passion for what you do. Then, live it every day.

Legendary Green Bay Packers Coach Vince Lombardi understood the importance of passion when he said, "Every time a football player plays the game, he's got to play from the soles of his feet to the top of his head. Some guys play with their head. That's okay, you've got to be smart to win. But more important, you've got to play with your heart, with every fiber of your body." Get excited about the ways you serve and give to others! Feel the positive emotion and put an attitude of passion into your service.

High tech service

Some say that personal service is next to impossible in today's hectic, fast-paced world. Actually, modern technology can make it easier to provide better service. Don Peppers is co-author (with Martha Rogers, Ph.D.) of the international best seller, *The One to One Future* (Doubleday Currency, 1993), and most recently, *Enterprise One to One* (Doubleday Currency, 1997). Peppers recently explained to my audience what he calls one-to-one marketing, in which you serve customers better by understanding and responding to their individual, personal needs.

If you went into a bookstore, and the bookstore proprietor said, "Mr. Smith, welcome back! Guess what, Elmore Leonard has a new novel out. I know you like Elmore Leonard, so I put it aside for you," you would remain loyal to that bookstore because it makes it simpler for you to find the books that you want.

The problem is, it's not very cost effective for the bookstore to do this. Even for a really, really good bookstore proprietor who might remember a hundred customers, those hundred customers are only going to account for 5 to 10 percent of that store's business.

Consider if you were to automate this process in some way! In fact, Amazon.com [the online bookseller] is not a bad metaphor for this kind of bookstore. When I go back to Amazon.com, they really do say, "Hey, Mr. Peppers, welcome back. Elmore Leonard has a new novel out!" And they do it for me and thousands, tens of thousands of other people. It's very old-fashioned marketing, but it has the potential to be extremely high touch.

Aside from the value inherent for business, relationship-building computer software designed to help you serve others better can help you in every part of your life. It can help you remember people's birthdays, their children's birthdays, their favorite restaurants, special events in their lives, their preferences in entertainment, their personal goals, and so on. This new technology can help you give more of yourself to others in all the relationships of your life. There is nothing artificial about using software to track these details, because what really counts is your own interaction with other people. The software provides nothing more than a convenient way to manage the details that can help you serve others better and give more of yourself.

Now it's your turn

The four steps to great giving will work for you no matter what your goals or plans for success: whether you are a teacher, a member of the clergy, a busy executive, a parent, an entrepreneur, or someone just building a relationship with another person. They will work for you in business whether you deal with one customer, one thousand, or one million. Using the four steps to great service, take a few minutes now and explore this path by writing down ways in which you can give your best to others.

- First, envision a scene where you provide a perfect experience for someone. How could you improve the ways you interact with others? Write down your ideas in the space provided on the following page.

- Second, how could you get closer to those you serve? Remember that complaints or criticism can teach you ways to improve. How can you solicit these ideas from those you serve? Capture your thoughts in writing now.

- Third, go beyond the Golden Rule. How can you give others the treatment you would expect to receive, then go beyond and give them more?

- Fourth, how can you build passion in how you serve others? Write down some ways you can add your emotions to this process. Follow through and complete this list now.

Ways I can give my best to others

_____

_____

_____

_____

_____

_____

Explore the path of serving others and discover the value in giving your best. It is a road well worth traveling, yet it is not often followed in today's world. Test this path and you will encounter relatively few on your special journey. Yet it is a path that can be immensely rewarding. Get the best by giving your best, starting today.

Today's journal

What mattered to me today:

_____

_____

_____

_____

_____

Coincidences, hunches, breakthroughs I experienced today:

_____

_____

_____

_____

New ideas I had today:

_____

_____

_____

_____

My thoughts, feelings, reflections on today:

_____

_____

_____

_____

Look within you

*When you connect to your source, you can create
anything you'd like to have in your life.*

—Dr. Wayne W. Dyer

Today's chapter explores the path that can lead you to an enlightened, and possibly miraculous, existence. By following this path, it is possible to achieve success beyond imagination. What is this wondrous path? Very simply, *meditation*. By "going within" each day and spending time quietly concentrating on your highest self, it is possible for you to transform virtually everything in your outward, physical world.

There is a definite spiritual aspect to this practice. Like some other paths in this book, this one may challenge your belief system. If you find it difficult to believe in God, or in the effectiveness of prayer, you will not be able to get the full benefits from this path. As the saying goes: If you believe, no proof is necessary; if you do not, no proof will suffice. Regardless of your personal beliefs, please explore this path with your mind wide open. More than any other, it has the potential to transform your life.

Meditation: key to success

If you have not tried meditation, you are missing a most profound and positive experience. Contrary to what some think, meditation does not mean making your mind a blank. It means concentrating on awakening your higher self while letting go of outside distractions and extraneous thoughts. You have already learned that sitting quietly and concentrating at the alpha level once or twice each day can bring answers to difficult questions. Regular deep meditation can speed you toward your goals, lower your level of stress, help you deal with crisis situations, and improve your relationships. Research has indicated it can also lower your blood pressure and even your cholesterol levels. But it can also do much more.

Great thinkers through the ages have said that all you seek can be found within you. Meditation is part of the teachings of Buddhism, Hinduism, Christianity, and Islam. Regular meditation forges a spiritual connection between your inner self and the universal power that is behind all things, but you don't have to join a religion to practice meditation.

As you explore this inner path, you may find yourself on a path toward spiritual enlightenment. Belief in a higher power comes on its own when one meditates deeply and regularly. You inevitably discover you have a natural connection to a higher power. Everyone has this connection within, but many have lost the ability to know it or tune in to it. Meditation opens this channel, which in turn opens the door to immeasurable abundance and fulfillment in your daily life.

Practice makes perfect

All this sounds almost too good to be true. With these many benefits, why doesn't everyone meditate? Perhaps for the same reason everyone doesn't exercise: It takes a little time and effort to see results. As with any new skill, meditation has a learning curve and it can take some getting used to if you have never experienced it.

Just as you must exercise consistently to gain physical strength and endurance, you have to meditate regularly to experience real rewards. However, it is not unheard of for beginners to have some wonderful experiences. Later in this chapter, you will learn some simple steps to begin meditation. Make the commitment to meditate every day for at least 60 days, because the results are not immediate. Your daily effort requires only the willingness to relax quietly, concentrate on clearing your mind of the noisy jumble of daily thoughts, and listen. Your goal is to forge a link with your higher self. This takes a little discipline, because you first must train your mind to stop roaming randomly.

Set aside at least 20 minutes starting today at a regular time for quiet meditation and self-reflection. Eventually, you will probably want to increase the time you spend in daily meditation. Also, read some books about meditation. The more you know about how to meditate, the more quickly you will see results.

Create your reality

Dr. Wayne W. Dyer (author of *Your Erroneous Zones, Real Magic,* and *Your Sacred Self)* is a believer in the effectiveness of meditation. He has practiced it for years, with rewarding results. He talked about it during a recent interview with me.

> *When you get on this path, you begin to have an awareness that you do have a capacity within yourself to manage the coincidences of your life. You have a lot more say in what shows up in your life, and who shows up in your life. You get control over circumstances, control over things like luck, you are able to heal yourself, and to perform at high levels. These are things that our conditioning has told us we can't do. Once you get on this path, it's a very fast track. It's like you almost do a somersault into the unimaginable, and that's what's been happening with me.*
>
> *Twelve years ago, I couldn't have even imagined taking time each day to meditate. Today, I can't imagine my life without it.*

Dyer's latest book, *Manifest Your Destiny* (HarperCollins, 1997), is a guidebook that teaches a meditation skill called *manifesting*. Manifesting is an ancient principle that makes it possible to literally attract your desires through meditation. No, this isn't a pipe dream! I have used Dyer's manifesting technique with excellent results. Also, he told me of many successes others have achieved through manifesting: a person stuck in a dead-end career who suddenly got a promotion, a seemingly infertile couple who had a baby, a major financial burden being unexpectedly lifted, and so on.

The impossible is possible

You may have read stories of Indian yogis or Buddhist monks who do seemingly impossible things: consciously raise their body temperature, slow their pulse and breathing at will, and such. *Yoga Journal* magazine recently reported on a modern Indian surgeon and yogi, Dr. Brahma Chari Jayant, who runs a school near Hardwar, India. Jayant gives public exhibitions of his special abilities gained through years of deep meditation and concentration. For example, he can relax comfortably as a two-ton vehicle drives over his chest. He can shatter light bulbs between the palms of his hands without cuts or pain. Certain yogis and monks can do these things, because they have connected with a reality beyond our everyday world. They have linked themselves to the spiritual force in them and in everything, and it allows them to do amazing things.

If you are willing to suspend your doubts and let it happen, you can tap this same universal force to bring you everything you want and need. There are probably things you desire that seem out of reach now. Manifesting through meditation can actually cause these things to come into your life, no matter how impossible this may seem to you right now.

Silence is power

The first step, Dyer told me, is to connect with your *source*. You might prefer to give this source a name, such as God, or simply the Universe. You reach this source through complete silence. Not silence of sound, but silence of thoughts. The way to achieve this silence is through meditation. I asked Dyer to explain how it works:

When you go to silence, you are literally making contact with your source, and it is from your source that all things in the physical world are created. The original quantum physicist was St. Paul. He said, "That which is seen does not come from that which does appear." So there is something in all physical things that is not of the physical world, and you have to find that. Most of us have really forfeited our ability to go back and forth between the world that we notice, and that invisible world that we create, and that's what manifesting is. When you meditate, you figure out a way to do this.

If this explanation is hard to grasp, do not be dismayed. A complete explanation of this metaphysical concept could fill many, many pages. In the simplest terms, you have to be willing to let go of the way you view reality and accept the fact that there is an invisible creative force that flows through you, through everyone else, and through everything you see around you in the physical world. On a subatomic level, modern physicists tell us that everything physical is actually made of pure energy. Not surprisingly, the enlightened ancients told us about this energy. It is the energy of what we call God, the universal source of power that holds everything together. This power is yours to freely use for any and all productive and worthy purposes while you are here on Earth.

Next, I asked Dyer to give the basic technique of manifesting in simplified terms:

I had a great teacher in India.... He asked me to teach this meditation. It's simply repeating the sound of God. There is the same sound and name for the Creator in every language...God, Allah, Buddha, Krishna, Yahweh. All of the names for the Creator in all languages have this sound.

This is the sound that you learn to repeat, because it's the sound of effortless perfection. As you make that your inner mantra, it begins to nourish your soul. And you can send that energy out into the world and literally understand that this invisible force is the source of all things. It allows tomato seeds to become tomatoes, and allows you to become who you are. The same energy that moves a thought across your mind moves a comet through the sky. That energy is in all things, which means there is no place where it is not.

This energy of creation that flows though you and me and everything else comes from the source of all creation. By focusing this energy with consistent intention on what you desire, these objects or people are literally drawn toward you and brought forth into your life. Yes, it sounds hard to believe, but it can work. Remember that words and sounds contain vast amounts of energy. Without words, little could be created in our physical world. Words are the bridge that carries our shapeless thoughts into physical form, and according to Dyer, the ultimate creative word is *God*. Repeating this universal word aloud with focused attention, in any language, can bring positive results.

Dyer suggests you give the manifesting technique a conscientious daily effort for a few months. For some people, it takes far less time for the process to bring rewards. Manifesting may be a big challenge to your belief system. Just have the willingness to keep an open mind and try it, and watch what happens. Along with Dyer's book, *Manifest Your Destiny*, you can try a short audio program he created that will guide you in this technique, *Meditations for Manifesting* (Hay House, 1997). Simply listen and follow along as Dyer explains what to do.

Manifesting can be a very powerful path to success. All it requires is the willingness to look within and give it a try for the many benefits it can bring you.

Try basic meditation

If you do not feel quite ready for Dyer's manifesting technique, do not dismiss the idea of basic meditation. Just take 20 minutes a day for quiet meditation, using the easy steps that follow. It's a time to still your mind and relax each day. Meditation can become a major factor in your success. Best-selling author and successful business owner Mark Victor Hansen told me he meditates regularly for the benefits it brings him.

I wouldn't live without it. I get up about 4 o'clock every morning and meditate.... I meditate from 4 to 5 and go back to sleep. The whole principle is what you in-picture, you out-picture. So if you really picture the good that you desire, whether it's a great family life, which I've got and I'm proud of, or you visualize your business, a good relationship with your spouse, with God...there's no limit to what you can do in this time of meditation. It's the inner work that causes the outer realization, in my experience.

Fortune 500 executives, superstar athletes, effective parents, and top performers in every walk of life meditate daily for the positive results they receive.

Getting set to meditate

Here are steps for basic meditation. First, choose a regular daily time to meditate. This conditions your mind to relax at a regular time, making it easier. For most people, this will be early in the morning and/or just before bedtime. Other good times are at noon, and in the evening around sunset, when you are home from work, but haven't yet eaten dinner. It's best to avoid meditating right after a big meal, as this makes it harder to concentrate, because your stomach is competing with your brain for energy. A daily routine of meditation at a consistent time of day leads to effective results.

Experts suggest you select a regular place for meditation, such as a corner of your bedroom. If possible, use this location exclusively for meditation. The routine time and place soon become cues for you, and help you enter a meditative state more quickly and easily. Here are the steps for effective meditation:

♦ First, set aside 20 minutes for this routine. Go to a quiet place.

♦ Second, sit quietly with your back straight and your hands in your lap. Do not lie down, as you may simply fall asleep. Sitting is the best position for meditation.

♦ Third, close your eyes, and breathe in. Slowly inhale while counting silently to 12. Hold the breath for a count of 12, then exhale for a count of 12. Do this a total of six times, then relax and breathe normally.

♦ Fourth, relax your entire body progressively, starting with your feet and moving to your legs, hips, abdomen, chest, hands, arms, shoulders, neck, and head, until you are fully and deeply relaxed. These steps help release all tension from your body, which will otherwise distract you from finding the inner focus you seek.

♦ Fifth, focus your mind on one single thing to quiet your thoughts. Some suggestions here include focusing on the sound and rhythm of your breathing (in and out, in and out); focusing on a single word such as "peace" or "joy" or even "God" and repeating it either softly or to yourself in time to your breathing; or focusing on a numerical count-down from 50 to one, and repeating as necessary. In each case, as the repetitive breaths, words, or numbers continue, let yourself relax more and more deeply. If other thoughts intrude, observe them, gently release them, and continue.

Some like to use the ancient mantra AUM (pronounced Om) to reach the meditative state. This works best if you slowly chant AUM, stretching it out as ohhhhhmmmmmmm, then pause, slowly inhale and repeat. Begin at a comfortable volume, but after a few minutes, lower your voice. Gradually keep lowering your voice until you finally are chanting AUM as a silent mantra within your mind. Give this method several weeks to really begin working for you. It is time-tested over centuries as an effective way to reach a state of deep inner awareness.

Focus on something

You might also try focusing on a visual object, such as a candle flame, a flower, or another natural object such as a seashell. When distracting thoughts enter your mind, gently let them go and return to your single focus of attention. You will gradually be absorbed into your inner silence. Meditation usually isn't a continuously deepening state. For most people, it is similar to gentle waves in the ocean, flowing between times of deep meditation and times of lighter meditation. With continued practice, the deeper times will become longer and more powerful, the lighter times shorter. Eventually, you will go deep enough to enter a very peaceful, serene place that is at the center of your being. It is here you make the superconscious connection that allows you to dramatically transform your outer world for the better.

Do not try to force your progress, just let it happen at its own pace. Be patient. Once you find the quiet place that is at your center, you will want to go there every time you meditate. This is where you will find answers, solve problems, visualize your desires and bring them to fruition, and in time discover your highest self.

Meditation has been described as a laboratory. Just as a scientist goes to a physical laboratory to experiment and see what works, so too will the meditative state give you a place to experiment with your inner self. Because you are a unique human being, you will have to practice and try new techniques as you meditate to see what works best for you. The rewards will be worth the time and effort you put into this practice.

Growing interest in spirituality

Inevitably, serious meditation connects you with spiritual power. Meditation and prayer actually go hand in hand, as both are ways to connect with a higher power. In recent years, more and more people are choosing to take this path. There appears to be a growing, global interest in spirituality. According to *Newsweek* magazine, more than half of all Americans pray on a daily basis, and nearly 90 percent of them believe God answers some of their prayers.

There is also a growing fascination with spiritual phenomena, such as angels, miracles, and visions. While Christianity and Judaism remain vibrant forces in the West, more people are being drawn to Eastern traditions, such as Buddhism and Hinduism. Recently, I discussed this trend with American-born Lama Surya Das, the highest ranking lama in the West. A Buddhist teacher and lecturer, Surya Das was born Jeffrey Miller. After graduating from college in the States, he moved to the Himalayas where he spent 25 years studying Buddhism.

We in the West have reached the apogee of technological and material development since World War Two. Particularly in America, people are still dissatisfied and are turning inward. The 70 million baby boomers have had everything they wanted in life. And still, many feel dissatisfied...and are looking for the meaning of their life. People are looking into spirituality— Western religions as well as Eastern religions, meditation, and Buddhism.

Moreover, as the millennium approaches I think there's going to be an upsurge, if not an eruption, in our collective psyche on many kinds of things. People are going to be looking in all kinds of directions. So I think it's very important for us to find something that is really wholesome, time-tested, and tried and true. For example, Buddhism is not just a new age phenomenon; it's older than Christianity and it has produced many, many enlightened masters over the ages.

Lama Surya Das has written a number of books, the latest of which is *Awakening the Buddha Within* (Broadway Books, 1997).

If you find yourself unexpectedly drawn to a spiritual path, do not be surprised. In recent years, more and more people seem to be discovering or rediscovering this timeless way to peace and enlightenment. Millionaire real estate developer and businessman Nick Bunick sat on the board of several corporations and founded several others. His life was filled with deal making and big business. The last place he expected to find himself was on a spiritual path. Yet, after having a series of remarkable angelic experiences, he has now fully committed himself to God. Nick Bunick's story is an amazing one. It's told in *The Messengers* by Julia Ingram and G.W. Hardin (Pocket Books, 1997). He talked about it with me in a recent interview.

The first time I had an angelic experience was on January 14, 1995. Prior to that, I honestly and truly did not believe in angels. I thought angels belonged in the same toy box as the tooth fairy and the Easter bunny. What is happening now is we are getting thousands of letters from people around the country who are having angelic experiences after having read The Messengers. *The angels are letting people know that God is intervening in their lives.*

As we approach the new millennium, it's very, very important that people realize that we should be living our lives according to the laws of God, which are very simple. They are, number one, that we have universal compassion in our lives; number two, that we have universal love; and three, that we live our lives in truth. Those are the three main messages received from the angels.

Of course, you can explore the spiritual path without having angelic experiences. Nor do you need to move to the Himalayas and become a Buddhist monk like Lama Surya Das. All it takes is your commitment to seek the higher source of power that is already within you. Most will agree that the best way to do this is through meditation. If spiritual enlightenment is your goal, you will improve your progress vastly by spending at least 20 minutes every day in silent meditation. Even if you have no interest in spirituality, meditation will help you succeed in virtually every area of your life.

The power in you

As mentioned earlier, when you get down to the level of infinitely tiny particles of matter, far smaller than the atom, you discover that the stuff that makes up everything in the physical world is composed of nothing but energy. In Eastern traditions, this subtle cosmic energy is called *prana* or *qi* (chi). You can become attuned to this energy and feel it actually flowing through you. With practice, it's even possible to control and move this energy through your body at will. Certain exercises, such as those of hatha yoga and t'ai chi, can help to strengthen and focus this energy flow. To illustrate how ancient these exercises are, consider that traditional yoga postures have been found in archeological stone carvings that are more than 5,000 years old. Recently, a scientist suggested that some of the angled poses of people seen in Egyptian carvings may actually be illustrations of yoga-like postures.

It is doubtful that the ancients carved yoga postures into temple walls to remind people to stay in shape! Nor were they placed there as a plan for stress-reduction, though that's a major reason many people practice yoga today. No, there has to be a far more profound reason these postures were once considered so important.

Energy exercises

Hatha yoga and similar exercises put the energy in your body into a harmonious, balanced state. With practice, you can learn to control the subtle energy within the body and make it flow gently upward along the spine to the brain. By doing this, you can greatly enhance your ability to reach deep levels of inner awareness in meditation. Eventually, through the use of these techniques plus devoted meditation, it is possible to achieve profound breakthroughs that go far beyond the scope of the everyday world. Such meditative insights enter into the highest realms of metaphysics and spirituality.

If these concepts sound intriguing to you, pick up a book or videotape and learn more.

You can practice yoga postures or other gentle stretching exercises before meditation and notice improved results. The great Paramahansa Yogananda, author of the classic *Autobiography of a Yogi* (Self-Realization Fellowship, 1946), created a set of special exercises for energy control that are very effective. You may come to understand why great civilizations of the past considered this inner energy so vitally important.

Making dreams come true

There is one more realm you may wish to explore on the inner path to success. It is the world of your dreams. No one really knows where dreams come from, although there are many theories. Nevertheless, it's a fact that dreams contain vast amounts of information. For some people, this information may be vital to success. There are countless stories of inspiration and breakthrough ideas from dreams. At least one Nobel prize winner attributes his award to the brilliant scientific idea he received in a dream. Author Robert Louis Stevenson claims that his writing ideas came from dreams. Recently, *Writer's Digest* told how novelist Jacquelyn Mitchard received the entire plot and all the character's names for her first book in an unusual dream. The book, *The Deep End of the Ocean* (Viking Penguin, 1996), became a major bestseller. While on tour to promote the book, yet another dream gave her the complete story for another best-selling novel. Dreams have also been said to contain prophecy, messages of healing, and even the voice of God.

Get the message

Mind control expert Jose Silva has said that dreams contain messages for us, but that we forget most of them quickly. However, it's easy enough to tune in to your dreams and capture their messages before they are lost. Keep a pad of paper and a pen by your bed and when you awake, immediately write down the details of the dreams you remember, nonsensical or not. Dreams usually communicate by allegory or symbolism. Days or weeks later when you review your dream log, the meaning of the dream will become clear. It's vital to make notes immediately, however, or you will forget the dreams. For some reason, dream memories dispel like mist in the morning sun.

You may think you do not dream. Experts say that everyone has dreams; it's just that some people don't remember them the next morning. To test this, set your alarm for, perhaps, 3 a.m., when normally you would be sound asleep. When the alarm wakes you, immediately jot down your thoughts. A strong affirmation before you fall asleep, such as "Tonight I will have a dream and I will remember it tomorrow," can also be effective. Tune in to your dreams and you can positively affect your waking state each day.

Finally, though your belief systems may have been tested by the ideas in this chapter, be willing to give these concepts a try. You may find them to be the most powerful paths to success of all.

Today's journal

What mattered to me today:

_____

_____

_____

_____

_____

Coincidences, hunches, breakthroughs I experienced today:

_____

_____

_____

_____

New ideas I had today:

_____

_____

_____

_____

My thoughts, feelings, reflections on today:

_____

_____

_____

_____

Live in the moment

Live in each moment completely, and the future will take care of itself.

—Paramahansa Yogananda

Welcome to the final day of the Countdown. You have a lot to be proud of, because you have stayed with the program all the way to Day 1. At the end of this chapter, you will have the chance to review all the paths to success you have explored over the last three weeks, and choose the ones that resonate with you. But first, let us explore one final path: *living in the moment*.

Every day has potential

Every moment of your time on earth is fleeting, one that will never come again. Each day that you are given is a day filled with opportunities and potential moments of greatness. Think about that. Each day is given to you only once, and once a day is gone, it never comes again. Let us assume the average human life span is 75 years. Some people live longer and some do not, but let's assume you will live at least that long. Those 75 years span a total of about 27,400 days. Of those 27,400 days in your life, how many will really count?

The greatest day of your life: today?

Will you remember today as one of the great days of your life? What about tomorrow? Will there be a day this week, this month, or even this year that you can make truly remarkable and memorable? You have the power to make one of those days contain a major personal breakthrough, a dramatic improvement in your life, or a really positive change in you. Will there be one day this week when you'll affect the life of someone else and make his or her life better? Will there be a day in the next year when you accept a major challenge to improve your life dramatically? You may think that great days don't happen so often, but the fact is, you make them happen through your actions. If you sit back and wait for those special days to come on their own, they rarely will.

Make every day count

Obviously you want to improve yourself, so consider this: If you're 20 years old, you've already lived more than 7,000 days. If you're 30 years old, you've already lived more than 10,000 days. Add about 3,500 hundred days for each decade beyond that. How many of those days have you lived at your highest potential, and how many days would you consider completely forgettable: the same old routine, including TV and a microwave dinner? When someday you look back over the days of your life, how many days will you be able to count as really great, really meaningful, really satisfying days?

Don't rely on tomorrow

At the end of their lives, too many people look back with regret at missed opportunities, at lost chances for improvement. Too many let time slip through their fingers by falling into a common trap summed up in, "There's always tomorrow." That would be true if you had an unlimited life span, if there were no accidents, no disease, no death. Of course, there *isn't* always tomorrow. Life is limited, and once it runs out, that's it. Life is to be lived, not wasted regretting the past, fearing the future, or letting the years pass you by. Successful people make the most of every moment they are given.

Now we know better

As mentioned earlier, physicists have discovered that all matter is made of energy. Interestingly, this mirrors the ancient beliefs espoused by great spiritual leaders. More recently in history, people doubted the energy concept, because they could not see it nor demonstrate it scientifically. Now that science has advanced some more, once again we know better.

The science of cosmology tells us that the world was created millions of years ago from swirling clouds of gas and in several hundred billion years our sun will exhaust its fuel and die, and the Earth will become a cold, dead rock with no life. There are those who feel that life will be no more, and that it doesn't matter because life is just a meaningless accident. Spiritual believers have a very different point of view. They believe life is extremely meaningful and important, and that we all are given free will to make the world a better place for all life. Further, they tell us that the manner in which we fulfill this daily quest on Earth *will* matter long after we have left our mortal bodies behind.

The hidden artist

Someone said that, when we see a beautiful piece of art, we know that an artist must exist who created that work. The artwork obviously did not form at random; there had to be an active intelligence at work to create it. How then can people observe the beauty of the world, its intricate systems in operation, along with the planets and stars all on course, and not imagine that there is an artist behind this magnificent creation? Today as in the past, these doubters are the ones who only believe in rational thinking. Someday, perhaps everyone will recognize the hidden artist.

If you do believe that a higher intelligence created our intricate universe, you may wonder if it has meaning. Again, spirituality provides a compelling answer: In addition to the growth of our own souls, we are put here to help others, to make the world a better place, and to pass the tests that each day brings. A powerful way to accomplish these goals is to *live in the moment.* In each interaction we focus on giving our best to others. When opportunities arise, we seize our chance to improve the world. As the unexpected lessons of life are taught, we learn from them. Dreaming of tomorrow or moping about yesterday can trap us in failure. Instead, we can access our highest self and reach success on this path through conscientious, steady focus on the moment at hand.

This isn't just an impractical pie-in-the-sky approach to life for dreamers. Consider Phil Jackson, the legendary coach of the world-champion Chicago Bulls, who consistently delivered record-shattering performances. When asked how he came up with the brilliant insight necessary to lead his team to victory after victory, he says that it came to him "in the moment." Jackson's book, *Sacred Hoops* (Hyperion, 1995) is a testament to the spiritual focus and mindfulness that led him to extraordinary success.

A what-if story

A man gets the bad news from his doctor that he only has one day to live. Of course, he's incredibly upset to hear this news. He goes home to tell his wife of his imminent demise and she asks him what he would most like to do during his last day. After a moment's reflection, he says that he would like to spend a few hours in meaningful conversation, then have a romantic, candlelit dinner with a bottle of good wine, and finally, go to bed and make love all night long.

"That's easy for you to say. You don't have to get up and go to work in the morning!" his wife says indignantly.

All of us have a little of both this man's and woman's point of view. On one hand, we want to make the most of each day, and close our eyes at night feeling fulfilled and complete. On the other hand, we're caught up in the daily demands of life, which leave little time for anything meaningful.

Get the right state of mind

Recall the limited-time state of mind introduced on Day 11 to help overcome procrastination. This same powerful state of mind can help you achieve positive, meaningful results each day. Get instant perspective on the importance of every day by thinking about it just like the man in the previous story. Ask yourself right now, "How would I live my life differently today if it was the last day of my life?" You would probably live it a lot differently. Ask yourself what changes you would make now if you had just one month or just one year to live, and then start making them.

Make it meaningful

If an average Joe knew he had just days to live, he'd probably try to find greater spiritual meaning. He would try to create deeper and more meaningful relationships, not just with his loved ones, but with everyone he knew. He would take time to teach his children some of the important things in life, so that they would have a greater appreciation for the beauty and magnificence that life has to offer. I don't know about you, but this sounds to me like a great way to live no matter how many days you have left!

Take a few minutes right now to answer some questions that will help you get this perspective. Jot down your answers under each question below. You may discover some ways to bring more meaning into your life starting today.

Think back over your life, and remember the few special people who had a positive impact on your growth and understanding. Right now, there is probably at least one person in your life—maybe more than one—who you could help in the same way. As you write down the answers to these questions, consider all the people in your life, your loved ones, friends, co-workers, and associates.

How many lives do you touch directly each day?

Of these people, who would benefit from greater encouragement from you?

Who would benefit from greater trust on your part?

Who needs more understanding from you each day?

Who would benefit from the enlightenment you could give?

Who would appreciate getting more respect from you starting today?

Who deserves greater love from you than you are now giving?

Is anyone you know trying to realize a dream? In what ways can you help?

As you consider ways to make a positive impact on the lives of those around you, do not ask for or expect anything in return. The advice and support you give unselfishly to others will automatically be returned to you many times over. The bottom line is, be the best you can be and help someone else be the best they can be. It is a simple formula, but it works.

Improve your interaction

One of the great ironies of life is that often people treat strangers better than they treat loved ones. They go out of their way to make guests feel comfortable and to flatter passing acquaintances, while taking those closest to them for granted. Ask yourself how you could interact better with others in your life.

Is there a friend or loved one in your life who would appreciate an unexpected compliment or sincere thank-you?

When was the last time you gave someone close to you a gift that wasn't expected?

Have you taken the time recently to listen patiently to someone's problems or concerns, without passing judgment?

If you had just one day to live, are there any close friends or family members you would treat differently? In what way?

Could you help a friend or loved one tomorrow by doing something for them without being asked? What could you do for them?

Improve yourself

Let us explore how you can improve how you deal with yourself. First, get perspective by imagining you have just a few short days to live. Then answer the following questions.

How would you change your life right now if you had just a few days to live?

Is there a personal challenge you would accept in your life?

Would you decide to forge a deeper spiritual faith with your Creator?

How would you improve an important relationship in your life?

Are there any people you would finally forgive for their past slights or angry words?

Would you communicate some really meaningful thoughts and ideas to your loved ones?

Would you truly appreciate the beauty and magnificence life offers each day?

What meaningful risk would you finally be ready to take in your life?

Author Aldous Huxley wrote, "There's only one corner of the universe you can be certain of improving, and that's yourself." With days to live, how would you make your corner of the universe better? By answering the previous questions, I hope you have discovered some ways to start doing this today. If you have given this exercise some thought, I'm sure your list touches some of your deepest truths, the things that are most important to you. Take action on these important things every day of your life. Do this starting today, and you will never have to look back with regret about not living your life to the fullest every day.

List the good stuff

Here is a final exercise to help you keep your perspective during the most hectic and frustrating days of your life. Create a list of all the good stuff in your life! It's fun and can make a difference in your future. For example, your list might include your friends and loved ones, such as your children. You might write down some precious memories, such as happy times when you were a child, a special vacation, or a romantic moment. Your list might include a place you love to go or something you love to do that gives you these positive feelings. You might list a brilliant thought or profound quotation. You may want to list a beautiful sight, a lovely fragrance, or a delightful taste. Your list may include something personally special, such as an experience you once had that somehow seemed perfect, spiritual experiences you've had, or other blissful and uplifting times in your life. Now, create your own list of peace, joy, and happiness.

Do not listen to doubt

You are an uncommon person. How do I know this? You have stayed with the Countdown to the end! Even if it has taken you longer than 21 days to get through it, you still have uncommon persistence. You will find within yourself all the motivation you need to achieve any goals you desire. Remember that every successful person has had doubts and fears.

The film they called a flop

Oliver Johnston was a young artist who helped create a full-length animated cartoon feature. Before the film even opened, it had been labeled a complete folly. Critics said it was sure to flop. On the night the film premiered, Johnston went to the theater completely doubting he'd even have a job the next day. Despite his fears, the film was a smashing success. Since it first opened, it has grossed nearly $300 million, won an Oscar, and has been acknowledged as a masterpiece. The film, produced by Walt Disney, was titled *Snow White and the Seven Dwarfs*. Before it was a proven success, there was plenty of doubt. Today, any doubts about such a wonderful movie seem completely ridiculous. If you have any doubts about success, they will one day also seem ridiculous to you.

The singer with no audience

During the early days of her career, a singer decided to give a free concert. She and her friends sent out hundreds of invitations all over town, inviting everyone to come to the performance. But when it came time for the show, the singer and her band were stunned and very disappointed. *Not a single person* had come to see them perform! Despite feeling shaken and very doubtful about her ability to attract an audience, the young vocalist refused to quit her dream. She stayed on her chosen path, and today, pop singer Amy Grant is a superstar with platinum albums and a shelf full of Grammy awards.

The company with no customers

A corporation was founded in a rented room with only a few thousand dollars of capital. The company's first product was an electric cooker that no one bought. As amazing as it seems now, this company's first product was an utter failure, and so was their second and third. Do you think the founders had severe doubts about the future? You bet they did, but it didn't stop them. Soon they introduced a small tape recorder, a product far more popular than their electric cooker, and the company took off. Within just a few short years, Sony Corporation grew to be an international force in consumer electronics.

Nearly every success began with the challenges of doubt and limitation. Problems of belief are more damaging than problems of technique. Do not let doubts, fears, or apparent limitations stop you from taking action to get the results you want.

You can do it

Be excited about how far you have come! If you have followed this course of self-exploration for 21 days, you have discovered new things about yourself. With this fresh insight, and with one or more intriguing paths to follow in the days ahead, you are on the verge of many exciting breakthroughs. Your personal path awaits you—but you will find it *only* if you keep moving forward.

It is not because things are difficult that we do not dare; it is because we do not dare that they are difficult.

—Lucius Annaeus Seneca

Imagine you are on a long journey to locate a magnificent lost city of riches. In your quest, you have already covered many miles of trackless terrain with a seasoned guide leading the way. At times, you felt much doubt about the routes chosen by your guide, but his apparent confidence kept you moving forward. Then, at long last, comes the moment you had dreamed of. After a long struggle up a winding mountain road, you and your guide reach the crest—and there in the distance, through swirling mists, you suddenly catch a glimpse of the road you seek. Yes, that's it! The path that will take you straight to the gates of the fabled city! But alas, your guide suddenly tells you he can go no farther with you. He must turn back to help others find their own paths. He encourages you to continue on alone, and says that other guides are ahead. These guides, he says, will appear as you need them. He tells you that everything will be fine if you just believe what he says, *and* if you keep moving forward. With that, he is gone. In the silence, doubt begins to fill your mind. You turn to look toward the road ahead, and now you aren't so sure it is the right one after all. A quest that once seemed so assured with your guide leading the way, now feels uncertain and risky. What should you do?

All glory comes from daring to begin.

—Eugene F. Ware

There is only one thing to do. You must move forward, and *become your own guide* until you discover the next one to guide you. If you hesitate and stay where you are, your momentum will be lost. The focus you have gained during the past weeks of your journey will be wasted. The energy for achievement you have built up will be scattered. Moving forward is the only way to achieve your dreams! And that is exactly what you must do the moment you finish this book.

They can because they think they can.

—Virgil

At the end of this chapter, follow through by reviewing all of the paths you've covered. Decide which path or paths resonate for you. By the way, don't expect this resonance to strike you like a bolt of lightning. The right path for you now may simply give you a good feeling or impart a sense of enthusiasm. Follow that feeling! Move forward on whatever path or paths inspire you, by turning to the Resources on page 247. Then pick up a book or tape, and explore further! Let this new information help you find the next guide along the way, who will direct you on toward your dreams. Stay in action and give your dreams of success a chance to become reality.

In the course of a lifetime, 21 days is a mere blink of an eye. Yet I hope sincerely the past 21 days will help make every future day of your life richer and more rewarding. It has been a real honor to be your guide as you have explored these different paths. I hope your quest for success is swifter and far more complete for our having spent this time together. Please write me at *Success Journal*, at the address at the back of the book, and share your personal success story with me. Whatever your goals may be in life, may you experience in abundance all the good things: happiness, good health, prosperity, fulfillment, and above all, the ultimate success you want in life.

Choose your path(s) to success

Once you have completed this chapter and its journal entry, you will have explored every path in the book. Then it's time to choose the paths you wish to explore further! You will want to check back through the daily journal entries you made over the past three weeks and review your notes. Look for significant instances where you felt on track, or times when coincidences and hunches seemed to happen. These are signs that you were tuning in to your higher self and getting on the right path.

Make summary notes on the following page.

Summarize your daily journal

Day/path description	Notes
Day 21 - Think about it	_____
Day 20 - Discover your destiny	_____
Day 19 - See your success	_____
Day 18 - Tell yourself to win	_____
Day 17 - Take charge of your life	_____
Day 16 - Simplify everything	_____
Day 15 - Celebrate and reflect	_____
Day 14 - Face your fears	_____
Day 13 - Take risks with confidence	_____
Day 12 - Turn failure into success	_____
Day 11 - Do it now	_____
Day 10 - Expand your horizons	_____
Day 9 - Learn from leaders	_____
Day 8 - Listen to your heart	_____
Day 7 - Plan for abundance	_____
Day 6 - Attract more money	_____
Day 5 - Focus your mind	_____
Day 4 - Make a real change	_____
Day 3 - Give others your best	_____
Day 2 - Look within you	_____
Day 1 - Live in the moment	_____

Once you decide which path (or paths) you want to explore further, turn to the resource section in the back of the book and follow through. Seek out the books and other materials that relate to those paths. These resources will lead you further down these particular paths. Do not expect to find all the answers in any one place. You may have to continue exploring and testing. You may get sidetracked, or find your path coming to a dead end. That's okay, because you have learned an important lesson! Simply back up and start over again on a slightly different path, and you will soon find yourself moving forward again. Think of this process as an adventure, and make it fun.

Your progress on your chosen path to success will probably involve constant testing. You will keep learning and growing, you will pass those tests and you will move forward again. Some of the tests will be the common obstacles of fear, risk, procrastination, and others we have covered here. Others will be new to you. That's okay, too. You can beat any obstacle with determination and understanding. There's a famous saying, "Success isn't a destination, it's a journey." So true! When you look back one day on the progress you've made toward your dreams, you will realize, as so many others have, that the experience of the journey was a priceless part of the reward.

You may find also that as you learn and grow, your definition of success will change. Perhaps you will find your goals changing, from external goals of wealth, fame, or glory, to inner goals of growth and wisdom. This is not unusual, and in fact it is one of the things that makes life so interesting! Just follow your heart's desire and take the path that works best for you.

After today, I invite you to continue your journal. Even if you only jot down a few words each day, it will be enough to help you realize and learn new things about yourself. Without a way to mark your progress, such as a daily journal, you won't clearly see your advancement along the path.

Life is truly a great adventure, and we live in an exciting time. Each moment offers us opportunity and growth. Each moment of your life, *live successfully!* Grow all you possibly can, thank your Creator for your existence, refuse to let anyone limit your ambitions, and above all, never stop following your personal path to success.

....

Today's journal

What mattered to me today:

_____

_____

_____

_____

_____

Coincidences, hunches, breakthroughs I experienced today:

_____

_____

_____

_____

_____

New ideas I had today:

_____

_____

_____

_____

_____

My thoughts, feelings, reflections on today:

_____

_____

_____

_____

_____

Resources

Use the following resources to help you further explore the paths you choose.

Day 21 - Think about it

The Magic of Thinking Big, David J. Schwartz, Ph.D. (Fireside, 1965)
Think and Grow Rich, Napoleon Hill (Fawcett, 1960)
Your Heart's Desire, Sonia Choquette (Three Rivers Press, 1997)
You'll See It When You Believe It, Dr. Wayne W. Dyer (Avon, 1989)

Day 20 - Discover your destiny

Taking Charge of Your Career, Nella Barkley (Workman, 1995)
To Build the Life You Want, Marsha Sinetar (St. Martin's Press, 1995)
What Color is Your Parachute?, Richard Nelson Bolles (Ten Speed Press, 1997)

Day 19 - See your success

The Joy of Visualization, Valerie Wells (Chronicle Books, 1990)
The Magic of Believing, Claude Bristol (Fireside, 1985)
The Power of Visualization, Lee Pulos, Ph.D. (Simon & Schuster, 1994)

Day 18 - Tell yourself to win

Affirmations of Wealth, V. John Alexandrov (Databooks, 1997)
I Deserve Love, Sondra Ray (Celestial Arts, 1983)
What to Say When You Talk to Yourself, Shad Helmstetter (Pocket Books, 1990)

Day 17 - Take charge of your life

Awaken the Giant Within, Tony Robbins (Fireside, 1992)
Goals, Setting and Achieving Them, Zig Ziglar (Simon & Schuster, 1995)
Psycho-Cybernetics, Maxwell Maltz (Wilshire Book Co., 1981)
Your Erroneous Zones, Dr. Wayne W. Dyer (HarperCollins, 1991)

Day 16 - Simplify everything

How to Want What You Have, Timothy Miller, M.D. (Avon, 1995)
Simplify Your Life, Elaine St. James (Hyperion, 1994)
The Simple Life, Amy Dacyczyn, et.al. (Berkley, 1998)
Simple Abundance, Sarah Breathnach (Warner Books, 1995)

Day 15 - Celebrate and reflect

The Greatest Miracle in the World, Og Mandino (Bantam, 1988)
A Promise Is a Promise, Dr. Wayne W. Dyer (Hay House, 1996)
Real Moments, Barbara DeAngelis (Bantam, 1994)
When All You've Ever Wanted Isn't Enough, Harold Kushner (Pocket Books, 1986)

Day 14 - Face your fears

Dare To Win, M. V. Hansen & J. Canfield (Berkley, 1994)
Hug the Monster, Leicester & Smith (Andrews McMeel, 1996)
Never Fear, Never Quit, Joe Tye (Delacorte Press, 1997)
Worry, Edward Hallowell, M.D. (Pantheon, 1997)

Day 13 - Take risks with confidence

The Book of Risks, Larry Laudan (John Wiley & Sons, 1994)
Live Your Dreams, Les Brown (Avon, 1994)
Making the Courage Connnection, Doug Hall (Fireside, 1997)

Day 12 - Turn failure into success

How High Can You Bounce?, Roger Crawford (Bantam, 1998)
Kicking the Procrastination Habit, Alyssa Haley (Thomas Nelson, 1992)
The Law of Success, Paramahansa Yogananda (Self-Realization Fellowship, 1980)

Day 11 - Do it now

Doing It! Peter McWilliams (Prelude Press, 1994)
Get It Done!, Ian McMahan, Ph.D. (Avon, 1996)
Maximum Achievement, Brian Tracy (Simon & Schuster, 1993)
Simple Steps to Impossible Dreams, Steven K. Scott (Simon & Schuster, 1998)

Day 10 - Expand your horizons

Charisma, Dr. Tony Alessandra (Warner Books, 1998)
Power Schmoozing, Terri Mandell (McGraw-Hill, 1996)
You Are the Message, Roger Ailes (Doubleday, 1988)

Day 9 - Learn from leaders

An Eye for Winners, Lillian Vernon (HarperBusiness, 1996)
Everyone's A Coach (audio), Shula and Blanchard (HarperCollins, 1995)
Mentoring: The Tao of Giving & Receiving Wisdom, A. Huang, et al. (HarperSanFrancisco, 1995)

Day 8 - Listen to your heart

Awakening Intuition, Mona Lisa Schultz (Harmony, 1998)
Intuitive Imagery, Pehrson and Mehrtens (BH, 1997)
Practical Intuition, Laura Day, et al. (Broadway Books, 1997)

Day 7 - Plan for abundance

Clicking, Faith Popcorn (HarperCollins, 1996)
Rocking the Ages, Smith & Clurman (HarperBusiness, 1997)
The Roaring 2000's, Harry Dent (Simon & Schuster, 1998)
Technotrends, Daniel Burris (HarperBusiness, 1993)

Day 6 - Attract more money

The Consumer Reports Money Book, Bamford, et. al. (Consumer Reports, 1997)
The Lazy Man's Way to Riches, Richard G. Nixon (Penguin, 1993)
The Richest Man in Babylon, George S. Clason (New American, 1997)

Day 5 - Focus your mind

The Achievement Zone, Shane Murphy, Ph.D. (Berkley, 1996)
Concentration: How To Focus for Success, Sam Horn (Crisp Pubs., 1991)
Flow, M. Csikszentmihalyi (HarperPerennial, 1990)
Focus and Win (audio), Chris Witting (*Success Journal*, 1997)

Day 4 - Make a real change

Change Your Mind, Change Your Life, G. Jampolsky, M.D. (Bantam, 1994)
Taking the Fear Out of Changing, Dr. Dennis O'Grady (Adams Media, 1994)
You Can Be Happy, Richard Carlson, Ph.D. (New World, 1997)

Day 3 - Give others your best

Do Unto Others, Abraham Twerski (Andrews McMeel, 1997)
How to Be a Help Instead of a Nuisance, Karen Wegela (Shambhala, 1996)
The Platinum Rule, Dr. Tony Alessandra (Warner Books, 1998)

Day 2 - Look within you

Autobiography of a Yogi, Paramahansa Yogananda (Self-Realization Fellowship, 1946)
How to Meditate, Kathleen McDonald (Wisdom, 1984)
Journey of Awakening, Ram Dass (Bantam, 1990)

Day 1 - Live in the moment

Even Eagles Need a Push, David McNally (DTP, 1994)
Living the Mindful Life, Charles Tart (Shambhala, 1994)
Peace is Every Step, Thich Nhat Hanh (Bantam, 1992)

Contact us

We would like to know how *21-Day Countdown to Success* has helped you, and would appreciate any suggestions or comments. You can contact us at:

Chris J. Witting, Jr.
The Success Journal Corporation
2516 Waukegan Rd., Suite 301
Glenview, IL 60025
Phone: 888-GOFORIT (463-6748)
Fax: 847-583-9025
e-mail: info@successjournal.com
www.successjournal.com

The Success Journal Corporation, founded in 1992, is a consulting, publishing, and media syndication company based in suburban Chicago. Our mission is to help others achieve personal and professional success. We strive to do this through inspiring, entertaining, and informative broadcasts, tapes, publications, and in-person presentations. Our subsidiary company, Creative Broadcast Consulting, helps authors and experts gain media exposure through direct mail, broadcast interviews and program syndication.

Chris J. Witting, Jr. is available for speaking engagements and for individual or corporate consulting. Please contact us for availability.

Index